The Vital Edge

Sporting Mindsets for Business
Performance

By Louis Collins, Ph.D.

The Vital Edge

First published in the United Kingdom in 2014

© 2014 by Louis Collins

ISBN: 978-1-291-78814-3

All rights reserved. No part of this publication may be reproduced, distributed, or transmitted in any form or by any means, including photocopying, recording, or other electronic or mechanical methods, without the prior written permission of the publisher. This book may not be lent, resold, hired out or otherwise disposed of by way of trade in any form, binding or cover other than that in which it is published, without the prior consent of the publisher.

Cover image: Courtesy of Fotosimagenes.org,
www.fotosimagenes.org/performance

Printed in USA by Lulu, Raleigh, N.C. USA

I am eternally grateful to my ever-patient and loving wife, Anne, for reading endless drafts, and to my son Andy for his invaluable advice, editing and proof-reading. I am also indebted to my two daughters, Beth and Georgi, both of whom have inspired and encouraged me in so many ways.

I must also thank my numerous blog followers, many of whom have provided me with encouragement, feedback and input to content that has found its way into this book.

The Vital Edge

Contents

INTRODUCTION 7

PART I   TEAMS & INDIVIDUALS 13

Chapter One   Winning Margins 14

Chapter Two   Personal Sacrifice 25

Chapter Three   Collaboration 34

PART II   THE GAME INSIDE 48

Chapter Four   Visualisation 49

Chapter Five   The Inner Game 57

Chapter Six   Playing the 'A' Game 67

Chapter Seven   Optimists Win 77

PART III   MOTIVATION 91

Chapter Eight   Breaking Barriers 92

Chapter Nine   Motivation........................ 101

Chapter Ten   In the Flow 112

PART IV   SPORTING KNIGHTS 127

Chapter Eleven   Identifying Talent.......... 128

Chapter Twelve   Half-Time Pep Talks.... 141

Chapter Thirteen   Marginal Gains............ 152

PART V   GOING BEYOND LIMITS...... 164

Chapter Fourteen   Riding on the Edge.... 165

Chapter Fifteen   Exploration................... 174

The Final Whistle... 186

References... 193

About the author 197

INTRODUCTION

Learning lessons from sport and applying them to the business world is certainly not a new idea. I suspect we've been drawing parallels between sport and 'real life' since the Ancient Greeks were strutting their stuff at Olympia, if not before. So, why write this book? What's new?

Well, for starters, I love examining what happens inside the sporting arena; observing athletes' ways of dealing with adversity; figuring out what makes the difference between two well-matched performers; wrestling with the relative balance between raw talent and hard-work when it comes to sporting success. Sport, with all its dramas and intrigue, team-work and single-mindedness, successes and failures, not to mention unpredictability, offers us more than just entertainment. It provides insights into psychology, neuroscience, group dynamics, team-building, performance, learning, development and personal growth. It is a ready-made social experiment being played out in public, where people's character, motivations and emotions are laid bare.

People in business, whether leaders, managers, supervisors or team members, can all benefit from lessons that emerge from the sporting world, particularly if they have any desire to be the best that they can be.

The Vital Edge

I write this book from a number of perspectives. First, from the position of a sportsman. I have enjoyed competing in a large number of sports throughout my life, most notably football, athletics and swimming. I have participated competitively, at national level, and socially, and have experienced both the joy of success and the disappointment of defeat. In addition to playing, I have also tried my hand at being a football coach. As I have grown older, and certain physical limitations have emerged, I have focused more on tennis, cycling and golf. I also write from the perspective of someone with an extensive executive career in the corporate world, where I experienced first-hand the approaches taken to identifying talent, training, performance management, reward and motivation. My final perspective is from that of a leadership development consultant and coach. I work with individuals and teams in business, and I frequently hear people make personal and emotional connections with sporting analogies. When discussions about teamwork, collaboration, or coaching emerge, the way that people relate, and make sense of what is happening in their environment, is often helped by reference to their favourite sport, athlete or team.

Fulfilling one's own personal potential lies at the very heart of the sports-person's world. An athlete's primary job is to run faster, jump higher or throw further. Put simply, they are all seeking *'the vital edge'*. But, it is now well-recognised that to be the very best, and to achieve the nano-second or millimetre margin that might make the difference between gold & **silver** (or even between qualification for the Olympic team and staying at home to watch it on TV) athletes need to understand a lot more than their traditional physical training programme. In the course of becoming the best they can be, they become well-versed in areas of muscle physiology, nutrition, anatomy, cardio-vascular mechanics, as well as some very important principles about the way their brain operates. They learn relaxation techniques, they learn how to manage and channel emotions, and they practice positive visualisation exercises.

And what is it we need and expect from our business leaders? Problem-solving, decision making, emotional intelligence, an understanding of what motivates people, an ability to engage and quickly establish rapport with others, conflict management and resolution, negotiation skills, an ability to manage their own emotions, an engaging communication style, and the list goes on and on…

It seems clear that having even a rudimentary understanding of the way the brain works, and the neuroscience that underpins our emotions, drives, moods and behaviours would be invaluable to anyone who counts even one item of this list of activities within their professional responsibilities. Why wouldn't someone who wants to be the 'best they can be' seek to give them self every advantage in achieving that vision? Sports people do. They are constantly seeking the 'edge' that might just put them on the top of the podium. Their physical body is 'the tool of their trade', but more and more of our top sports people are recognising that the brain is the 'executive' that's in control. The brain is the tool of the executive and business leader. Why would they not take the opportunity to gain a greater understanding of how it works and fine-tune their performance? Why would they not want to give themselves that vital edge by learning more from what emerges from the sporting arenas around the world?

The book is divided into five parts. Part I focuses on the contrasting dynamics of team and individual sports and the different qualities that are tested in each case. Part II dives deeper into the mind of the individual while attempting to perform at their best, and explores some of the positive ways that sportspeople have found to overcome their own internal demons. Part III concerns itself with the important role that motivation plays in performance, both from an internal and external perspective, as well as the important principle of 'flow' in achieving peak performance. Part IV then turns its attention to the role of leadership by looking through the eyes of three very different sporting giants who have achieved great success as coaches. And finally, Part V asks what can be learned from those people who choose to go beyond limits, stretching and challenging themselves in ways that most of us would never consider.

My intention is that you enjoy the sporting anecdotes, that you will find inspiration in at least one of them, and that some of the insights revealed throughout the book, will help give you a sporting chance of discovering your *'vital edge'*.

The Vital Edge

PART I   TEAMS & INDIVIDUALS

The following three chapters explore teams & individuals in sport. I love the fascination and contrast between how sport is played out in individual versus team sports. In tennis (singles), golf and boxing, we have tremendous tension that often rises to gladiatorial levels. The loneliness and isolation of the tennis player in the grand slam final, calls for a highly focused brain. Yes, there may be coaches in the stands, or seconds in the corner of the ring, but in the thick of the action it is a raw one-on-one battle. Sometimes a physical battle, but often a battle of wits and psychology.

Team battles highlight different facets. Collaboration, communication and leadership. The very best teams when completely in sync, appear to play with what resembles telepathy.

We play as part of a team in business, but we often find ourselves on our own, having to make decisions, manage conflict, and our own internal demons.

We can learn much from both.

Chapter One   Winning Margins

The story of unassailable leads

On one amazing weekend of sport in July 2012, two elite sportsmen with what appeared to be unassailable leads experienced quite different outcomes and emotions. One went on to complete the job, and put himself into the history books, while the other, sadly, suffered a 'meltdown' as he saw the finishing line in sight.

What can we learn from these two events, and what was going on for these two athletes at those crucial moments?

Adam Scott, a hugely talented Australian golfer, led *The Open* (*sometimes known as 'the British Open'*), one of Golf's four major championships, by a very comfortable margin on the final day's play at Royal Lytham & St. Annes. If he were to defend the lead he had skilfully carved out over the previous three days, it would be his first ever 'Major' triumph. At one point he held a 6 shot lead, and no-one in the rest of the field was making any serious inroads. One or two players made the occasional threat, only to falter again at the next hole. Meanwhile, Scott played like the ice-man. He was focused, calm and very much playing *'in the present'*. He was not getting excited and was playing a very safe game, staying out of all trouble. With 4 holes to go, he still held a

4 shot lead. Up ahead of him on the course, Ernie Els, the popular and experienced South African, with previous Major wins to his name, was quietly picking off the occasional birdie on the back 9 holes, but none of the TV experts and commentators, nor the crowd, foresaw what was about to happen. Scott, who hadn't put a foot wrong during the 4 days of intense play, dropped 4 shots by bogeying the last 4 holes. Els, from nowhere, was The Open champion. The crowd and TV audience were stunned.

At almost exactly the same time, 500 miles further south, cycling history was being made in Paris. Bradley Wiggins, the enigmatic British cyclist, became the first man from his country to ever win the Tour de France in its 99-year history. Wiggins had held the iconic yellow (leader's) jersey from very early in the 3 week long race, and his lead had been considered unassailable for the previous 4 or 5 days. Only after the penultimate day's racing, when Wiggins reinforced his lead, did he allow himself the luxury of acknowledging that, barring a disaster, victory would be his in the Champs Elysees. But, he still had work to do on the final day, and his focus was concentrated on helping his team-mate, Mark Cavendish, to win the final stage. He was successful in this, setting up Cavendish for a final sprint finish that saw him race to his fourth stage victory in four years in Paris. A short while later, Wiggins stood on the top step of the podium to be crowned the 2012 Tour de France champion.

Success, and staying focused, depends hugely on being able to quieten the 'inner voice' **(The Inner Game of Work, 2000, Tim Gallwey [Ref 1])**. Avoiding the twin enemies of success (regret and anxiety) is vital if you are to play your best game. None of us can be sure what Adam Scott was experiencing as his bogey count rose during those final few holes, but I am willing to bet that one of two thought processes were dominating his brain at that time. He was either playing the game of 'Regret', reflecting on the 'bad' choices of shot he had just made, or the game of 'Anxiety', worrying about how he was going to play his next shot and recover from the 'bad' shots he had just played. One or other (or both) of these distracting, and very lonely, inner games was being played out, all by himself, and in full view of a global audience, meaning that, on this occasion, he was unable to come through and take the big prize.

Wiggins' inner game was played to perfection. He permitted himself only a very brief moment of anticipating his victory, before refocusing his attention on the task of helping his team-mate to a final-day stage victory.

Sport, and business, is littered with examples of people grabbing defeat from the jaws of victory. These moments are described variously as; losing focus, coming up short, being frightened of winning, over-thinking, believing you've already done enough. When things begin to unravel in these situations, it inevitably proves very difficult for people to recover and get back into the state that had been working so well.

Of course, it can be dangerous to draw too many comparisons between cycling and golf. The Tour is a three-week long event with the focus on the team and extreme physical endurance. The Open, on the other hand, is a test of the individual, is much less physically demanding, but does demand extreme concentration and focus each and every time a stroke is played.

So, what learning can be extracted from the amazing Tour de France victory achieved by Bradley Wiggins and his team?

Team-work   Watching Team Sky operate in the Tour was fascinating. They functioned like a well-oiled machine, exchanging positions with monotonous regularity, and ultimately focused on one thing – to get Wiggins into position, stage after stage, day after day, over a three-week period, to accumulate a lead that would ultimately secure the *'maillot jaune'* for the team. Each rider had a different role to play, and they stuck to it. Some of the riders are referred to as *'domestiques'* (servants) whose role is to ride at the front, shielding team-mates from the wind and airflow, allowing them to preserve energy for later in the race. The team members were completely selfless in the way they worked. Egos (and there were plenty) were put aside, for the benefit of the group. There were people in the team who could have sought their own individual glory, but they worked for something bigger – the team. Wiggins was always quick to acknowledge his team-mates and their role in putting him in the position to lead and win the race for the team.

Adaptability   Wiggins had transformed himself physically to make a serious assault on the Tour. He already had a successful career as a track cyclist with 6 Olympic medals to his name. But, to win the Tour de France is the ultimate prize for road cyclists, and demands extensive all-round attributes. It requires an ability to climb punishing Alpine peaks, to have unparalleled endurance, speed when required, as well as tactical nous and patience. Wiggins lost weight and changed his body shape over a number of years, in order to adapt to the demands of this unique event.

Learning from Experience   Wiggins had suffered disappointment and failure in previous events. Most recently, in 2011, he broke a collar bone early in the race and had to withdraw. In 2012, that learning was invaluable. Despite a large number of crashes and pile-ups, Wiggins stayed out of trouble and was always well shielded by the team, like bees in a colony protecting the queen.

Discipline   Wiggins and the team remained focused, calm and disciplined throughout the event. They had a plan and they stuck to it. They were prepared to allow other teams to win stages and sprints, always remaining focused on the big prize which was the yellow jersey at the end of the overall event. They could have panicked or worried about losing ground and deviated from the plan, but their belief in the plan and discipline in executing it was unwavering.

The significance of Margins   After more than 87 hours of gruelling pedalling, Wiggins' margin of victory over the nearest rider was a mere 3 minutes. Sir David Brailsford, the Performance Director of British Cycling and Manager of Team Sky, advocates an ethos of 'aggregation of marginal gains' (*A Winning Advantage, Sky Pro Cycling)*, [Ref 3]. He encourages the entire team, not just the riders, to seek an extra 1% in everything that they do, the theory being that if every member of the team can squeeze their own small improvement out of whatever their job is, the accumulative effect will be significant for the team. This means support mechanics switching wheels on bikes marginally faster, drivers of support vehicles issuing instructions sharper, drinks and food distributors finding marginally more efficient ways to get supplies to the riders. It all adds up, and any one of these could make the winning difference.

Learn from the Outside   Another innovative way of thinking introduced by Brailsford is the way he has opened up his cycling team's approach to people from outside of the sport. He has actively sought challenges to assumptions about 'how things are done around here'. Cycling has a long history, and there is a tendency, like in many established sports, as well as businesses, to assume that the people on the inside know best. He has been met with criticism by some within the sport for being so bold as to invite outsiders in, but, having people from totally different disciplines looking at training methods and racing formations, and questioning established practices, he has been able to introduce new ideas and fresh thinking, and protect his riders from complacency and stagnation.

We will return to a number of these themes, and explore some in greater detail, in later chapters. In the meantime, I suspect that any business seeking to establish a recipe for success, could benefit from incorporating these five core principles into their modus operandi; **Teamwork**, **Adaptability**, Disciplined focus on **Planning**, Seeking **Marginal Gains** and **Learning** from both the inside and the outside of their business.

And, what happened to Adam Scott? Well, he held his nerve to win a tense play-off in the 2013 US Masters, demonstrating that he had learned from his previous experience, and won not only his first major championship, but also his own inner game.

CHAPTER ONE KEY LEARNING POINTS

- Play in the present
- Quieten the Inner Voice
- Adapt to survive & thrive
- Learn from both personal experience and from outside your field of work

CHAPTER ONE REFLECTIONS

At the end of each chapter you will find a set of 'ponder' questions.

You may want to keep a pencil handy as you work your way through the book as you can use these questions to reflect and note down any immediate thoughts that come to mind.

You may also wish to make additional copies of these sections for use in team meetings or group workshops to provoke wider dialogue and interaction.

How much more effective could teamwork be within your organisation? List some of the first things that come to mind.

_____

_____

_____

_____

_____

_____

_____

How adaptable are you and your people to strategy / market focus / industry direction / personal skills development? List a few examples.

_____

_____

_____

_____

_____

_____

_____

How much do you exploit all the sources of learning available on the outside of your organisation and even outside your industry? List some examples.

_____

_____

_____

_____

_____

_____

_____

Chapter Two   Personal Sacrifice

The Steeplechase Story

In the previous chapter, I drew some contrasts between a golfer who was very much playing and competing for himself, and a cyclist who was one cog in a well-drilled team. While each was always playing their own inner game, regardless of whether they were working alone or as part of a wider cause, there were clearly different dynamics operating in each case. Let's look now at a heart-warming story of compassion, a quality that is rarely highlighted within the competitive world of sport.

The history of track & field athletics exudes epic tales of sheer brilliance, endeavour, physical extremes and no shortage of heartbreak. Great names trip off the tongue, from Roger Bannister to Usain Bolt, from Jesse Owens to Mo Farah. One thing that typifies the top athletes is their absolute single-mindedness and focus. They live, eat, sleep and breathe their event, to the point of obsession, giving up a great deal to be the best they can be, including careers and social lives, in a supreme effort to occupy top spot in their chosen discipline.

Which is what makes the story of the European Athletics Championships, 3,000m Steeplechase final in 1994, all the more fascinating. The championships were held in Helsinki, and were run as a team event, with points awarded to countries according to individual representatives finishing places in finals. The Italians possessed a very strong team, including former world champion, Francesco Panetta, and defending champion Alessandro Lambruschini. Panetta was a fiery character, and, when asked the day before the race whether he would work with the other Italian runners to secure team victory, he made it clear he was going to run his own race. He was reaching the end of his career, and most pundits gave him little chance of securing one of the top spots. Furthermore, it was unlikely that there would be many more opportunities for him to win a medal in a major championships again.

As the race developed, and the runners settled into their pace and jostled for position, Lambruschini, the favourite, tripped and tumbled over a hurdle, falling awkwardly onto the infield. Panetta had a golden opportunity open in front of him. With Lambruschini in difficulty, he could have taken full advantage by mounting a serious challenge for that final medal of his career. What happened, though, was truly inspiring, and restores one's faith in human nature. Panetta, stopped, turned, and helped his countryman to his feet. Clearly shaken and hurt, Lambruschini was in no state to make an immediate dash to catch up with the rapidly disappearing pack. Panetta now took on the role of pacemaker and motivator. He slowly but surely nursed Lambruschini back in to the race, with regular encouragements such as "Come on, it's nothing, you can still win this thing", and

"It's alright, don't panic". "Don't start sprinting too early, we can pull them in gradually, and you can still win", he urged.

Lambruschini did indeed come back to win gold, in a momentous race, with a late surge for the line. Panetta eventually finished in eighth place (out of twelve runners), following his own stumble over a fallen runner in the final lap, while trying to mount his own final push for a medal. He played the whole episode down after the race, refusing to be seen as a hero, dwelling only on his own failure to secure a medal in that final push for the line. [Ref 4].

The personal sacrifice that Panetta displayed when he totally discarded his personal race plan in favour of working for the success of his colleague and, let's not forget, fellow competitor, is truly inspiring. Knowing how much athletes care about their own performance, and how much effort they put in over months and years for those rare chances of glory, it makes it even more remarkable that, in an instant, in the middle of the race, he reverted to being a caring, supportive, motivating colleague, willing to give up his own personal shot at winning, for the good of his team-mate and his country as a whole.

We will probably never know what went on in his head at that moment, but my guess is that he instinctively felt that there was something 'bigger' than his own personal success at stake. He may have calculated in an instant that team points were at risk, and it was important for the good of his Italian team to help get his colleague back in to the race. He may have figured that Lambruschini stood a better chance than him of winning gold, even from the difficult position he was now in at the back of the field, and that the team would be better off having them work together rather than against each other. Or, perhaps it was simple human compassion that caused him to stop, help and change his plan.

Team-work, in any walk of life, but most notably in business, can be a tricky affair. What actually makes a good team, and how do you know when a team is functioning optimally? The classic list of qualities that contribute to great team-work, typically include, **reliability, constructive communication, active listening, willingness to share, flexibility and respectfulness**. While not an exhaustive list, by any means, it is rare to find *'prepared to suffer personal pain or loss for the good of the team'* as a key quality cited as a requirement of team members.

The optimistic set of ingredients for building an effective team can take you so far, and, so long as major conflict, or unplanned challenges, do not occur, may prove to be successful. However, in an ever more challenging and complex business world, the reality is that the stresses and tensions placed upon teams is such that, one of the key predictors of a team's success is how well team members collaborate, particularly at times of conflict, and when plans go wrong, as they inevitably will.

Collaboration is an often misunderstood and overused term. It has been fashionable for companies to place it at the centre of their 'desired' culture and as one of their 'highest-prized' employee values, but it is often diluted to mean little more than 'good teamwork' or 'co-operation'.

But spotting true collaboration can be a rarity within corporate and public service cultures. It demands a high level of self-awareness and skill at spotting and managing varying personal styles by all team members. It takes hard work and patience, a recognition of where effort is required, and it calls for a very high level of openness and honesty. When embraced, practised and role-modelled throughout an organisation, people learn, develop and grow, resulting in more engaged, effective and productive teams. Collaborating teams recognise that there is a bigger prize at stake than simply the sum of the individual parts. There is no internal competing within the team, and no working against the bigger vision for personal glory. Personal egos are set aside, and people are prepared to 'take one for the team'. *(Thomas-Kilmann Conflict Mode Instrument),* [Ref 6]

Collaboration within teams is not simply about compromise or agreement for an easy life. Great collaborators are highly assertive and, unlike internal team competitors, who speak the language of team-work, but are more interested in achieving their own agenda, they cooperate effectively and acknowledge that everyone's input is important. They actively seek out a variety of viewpoints to get to the most appropriate solution, and are not interested in compromising on a trade-off simply to move things forward. Collaboration is even more important when 'high-quality solutions' are required, something that is becoming ever more important in an increasingly uncertain and complex business world where creative thinking is at a premium.

CHAPTER TWO KEY LEARNING POINTS

- Personal sacrifice and the greater good
- Attributes of successful team-work and co-operation
- Collaboration is more than merely compromise and agreement

CHAPTER TWO REFLECTIONS

Think about the best teams you have been part of. What set them apart? List those characteristics that made them special.

_____

_____

_____

_____

_____

_____

Were people prepared to put personal aspirations on hold for the benefit of the team? What about teams you're part of today? Write down examples where you have seen it work well and/or badly.

_____

_____

_____

_____

_____

_____

_____

How confident are you, that when the 'race plan' fails, your colleagues will respond solely for the good of the team? Capture any examples where this has happened or failed to happen.

_____

_____

_____

_____

_____

_____

_____

Chapter Three   Collaboration

Barcelona and Pelotons

In the previous chapter I asked you to think of the best team you have been part of, and what set it apart.

When I think of great teams in the world of sport today, my mind immediately shifts to Spanish football, and particularly Barcelona. I have no doubt that the 'Barca' team of the past four or five years will go down in history as one of the greatest football teams ever assembled. They have won around 20 competitions, both domestic and international, since the year 2000, and have been consistently ranked number 1 by both the European and International football associations during that period. They have also contributed a large quota of players to the Spanish national team, the current holders of both the European and World football titles.

So, what is it about Barcelona that marks them out? They may well be the most analysed team in the history of football, and I dare say every pundit has their own view of what makes them special, but the list of qualities that I want to highlight also have enormous significance for anyone seeking to build an effective team in the business world.

Knowing the system Every player in the Barcelona family, from the highest paid star, such as Lionel Messi, to the youngster in the youth academy, understands the philosophy, vision and system of play. The so-called *'tiqui-taca'* system (short, rapid passing, with constant interchange of player positions) is the established pattern of play adopted for the club. The young players are drilled in it from an early age, and new players who are signed for the club are recognised and selected for their ability to be able to fit the system. Commitment to this vision and philosophy of operating has been a key component of their success.

Flexibility & Adaptability As a result of the style of play and the level of familiarity everyone throughout the club has with it, they are able to interchange roles and positions seamlessly. When injuries occur, the players who are drafted in as replacements slot into the team effortlessly. On those rare occasions when players lose the ball or are caught out of position, team-mates are able to slot into their role without feeling unfamiliar in that position.

'Telepathic' understanding The level of understanding that is displayed between members of the Barcelona team, when they are in full flow, certainly makes it look like telepathy is at work. They pass the ball into areas without looking, knowing exactly where their team-mates will be. They weave shapes at speed with the ball and their movement, baffling the opposition with an uncanny awareness and anticipation of each other's movements. Watching Xabi, Iniesta and Messi when operating on this level, is like watching a ballet.

What could be achieved in business with a team where everyone clearly understands and is aligned with the vision, where every team member is flexible and adaptable to the extent that they know each other's jobs intimately, and where everyone has a relationship with each other that means they know exactly what each other wants, to the point where they are able to anticipate what needs to happen next?

In 2011, Cap Gemini suggested that in excess of 80% of CEOs highlighted 'idea sharing' as key to innovation, but only 16% admitted to having the right culture in place to allow it to happen effectively. In a similar vein, General Electric's 2012 survey of the world's top marketers revealed that 86% of them see collaboration as vital, but only 21% felt able to build such a culture successfully *(GE Innovation Barometer, 2012,* [Ref 5]*).* So what is it that makes it so hard for businesses to create the conditions for effective collaboration?

In the last chapter, I raised the importance of understanding collaboration, and being clear on what true collaboration entails, and can deliver. Let's look at this in some more detail. Kilman et al [Ref 6] describe a number of ways that people typically operate under competitive circumstances. Very rarely are the conditions right for collaboration to be the chosen mode of operation. Let's take a look at other ways that people in teams typically resort to behaving under conditions of conflict, stress or serious competition.

Avoiding *Acting in a way that does not address the issue directly.* This style is typified by delegating controversial decisions, accepting default decisions, and not wanting to hurt anyone's feelings. It may be a viable style to adopt when the issue and the relationship are of very low importance, but avoiding a serious issue may make the situation intensify, possibly damaging relationships further.

Accommodating *Involves accepting the other party's position or interest at the expense of your own.* People who naturally adopt this style are not assertive but tend to try to be more cooperative. It may be an appropriate approach when the issue matters more to the other party and when peace is more valuable than winning. It can, however, be counter-productive as you may be seen as weak, especially if used repeatedly. Furthermore, constant 'accommodating' may lead to increased personal stress.

Competing *Working to have your position or interests take priority over those of the other party.* People who tend towards a competitive style take a firm stand, and know what they want, usually operating from a position of power (whether position, rank, expertise, or persuasive ability). It can be useful in an emergency when a decision needs to be made fast; or when defending against someone who is trying to exploit the situation selfishly. However it can leave people feeling bruised, unsatisfied and resentful when used in less urgent situations. It is also not a useful style when it is important to generate diverse ideas or multiple solutions.

Compromising *Involves each party giving and getting a little in terms of position and interests.* People adopting a compromising style seek solutions that will to some extent satisfy everyone. This approach depends on everyone being prepared to give up something. It can be useful when the cost of conflict is higher than the cost of losing ground, when equal strength opponents are at a standstill and when there is a deadline looming. It is unlikely to work successfully for issues of principle and may cut off opportunities for collaborative problem solving.

Collaborating *Parties attempt to meet all or most of the interests underlying their respective positions.* Collaborators can be highly assertive, but unlike the competitor, they cooperate effectively and acknowledge that everyone's input is important. This is the most useful style when it is important to bring together a variety of viewpoints to get the best solution; when there have been previous conflicts in the group; or when the situation is too critical for a simple trade-off. It is most effective for generating 'high-quality solutions' but requires a very high level of trust between parties, and relies on the use of considerable interpersonal skills (e.g. it is vital to confront issues directly without threatening the other party). For some situations it may not be appropriate due to the fact that it can take considerable time and effort to implement.

Even though a collaborating mode sounds 'ideal' to most people, it may not always be the most appropriate approach in every situation, and the effort required in making it work successfully may not be worth the likely return. This is as true in business as it is in sport. In fact, when people are faced with overwhelming stress, they don't tend to have the mental clarity to engage in productive collaboration, resorting instead to one of the other default modes. This could show up as an outright competitive mode, resulting in an all-or-nothing dash for the line, in an attempt to win at all costs. Or, it might reveal itself as an accommodating style, particularly if the body is drained of energy, and the effort required to put in a final push feels like too much.

One of the best examples in sport where fierce competitors collaborate is in the world of cycling. Watching a *peloton* (the main body of cyclists in a road race) in action is a fascinating study in collaboration. The peloton travels as a pack, but individual riders take turns in riding at the front, allowing the riders behind to benefit from reduced headwind. Depending on the weather conditions, the peloton will take on a variety of different shapes, sometimes resembling a flock of birds flying in formation. Cycling within the protection of the main body of the peloton has been scientifically proven to require around 30% less energy than being at the front. For this reason, a peloton of riders can travel faster and further than any one of the riders could on their own.

When this becomes really fascinating in a major race, is when a breakaway group of, say 7 or 8 riders, make a strike for the finish. The timing of this is vital, as the riders in 'the breakaway' know, that given enough time and distance, a peloton of 50 will chase down, and re-absorb, a small group. But, if the group can make their move with a sufficiently small distance to go, and, more importantly, work efficiently and collaboratively as a mini-peloton, they will give one (but only one!) of their number a real opportunity of winning the race.

Generally, in sport, there can only be one winner. The benefits of teamwork and collaboration in cases like Barcelona are easy to see. If everyone plays their part, then the whole team benefits, and success follows.

Even in the case of Panetta and Lambruschini, it could be argued that Panetta gave up personal glory to give himself a better chance of being part of the overall success of an Italian team victory.

It is less simple to explain the depth of collaborative behaviour displayed by a small number of riders, all from different cycling teams, who find themselves 2 Km from the line, with the peloton only 30secs behind and closing fast. Only one can win, but they each know that the best chance they have of it being them, is to work together, to take their turn at the head of the group to push with all their might, even though their lungs are bursting and their calves feel like they are exploding. Resorting to riding their own race, to make their own dash for the line too early, would be disastrous for their own chances, and probably the rest of the lead group too. Only total collaboration will keep them ahead, and allow one of their number to win the race with a final sprint for the line.

It is little wonder that the fraternity and camaraderie displayed by competing cyclists on a tour is high. When you know that your success may depend hugely on collaborating with your fiercest rival in tomorrow's stage, then qualities of respect, trust and openness become all important. This is no less true for successful collaboration in business.

CHAPTER THREE KEY LEARNING POINTS

- Knowing the system
- Flexibility & Adaptability
- 'Telepathic' Understanding
- True collaboration

CHAPTER THREE REFLECTIONS

How much more sharing of the leadership burden might be possible in your business? List areas where this is possible.

_____

_____

_____

_____

_____

_____

What can you and your teams learn from the psychology of the peloton? Capture any examples that make sense.

_____

_____

_____

_____

_____

_____

_____

What conditions do you see as being most important to allow collaboration to flourish in your business?

_____

_____

_____

_____

_____

_____

_____

What have you seen getting in the way of allowing true collaboration to succeed? List any examples.

_____

_____

_____

_____

_____

_____

The Vital Edge

PART II   THE GAME INSIDE

In the next series of four chapters we will explore the importance of what is going on inside the head of sportspeople, and how mastering the 'inner game' is key to performing at your very best. This is as true in business, and indeed any walk of life, as it is in sport. Sport provides us with a tremendous arena to examine how this game works. Centre Court at Wimbledon can sometimes resemble a Skinner Box, an elaborate social experiment with the players (and all of their strengths and demons) laid bare for public examination. We thrill in the reactions of the players to both external and internal stimulation. We see superstitious rituals and tics in glorious HD. We are fascinated to see how one player's over-exuberance will either inspire or anger their opponent. How an encouraging roar from the crowd can either spark them out of a slump to lift their game to new heights, or add further pressure to their already heavy shoulders. When it comes down to two equally matched opponents in the skills stakes, it is this game, 'the inner game', that decides the winner.

Chapter Four   Visualisation

I am the Greatest

Dare to dream, and dream big. The irony of our brains is that, at one and the same time, they **are remarkably sophisticated interconnected wonders of nature, and rudimentary biological organs, with neurons that fire in similar ways whether the experience is real or imagined.** We can take advantage of this fact, by 'fooling' the brain with dreams and visions. The more elaborate and 'real' we make our dreams, the more connections and neural pathways we create. The more we rehearse the dream, the more chance of it becoming a reality. The more times we have lived the dream in our heads, the more prepared we are to face the challenges and take the opportunities that arise when we eventually get to live the dream for real.

Sportspeople know this phenomenon well. They use positive visualisation techniques alongside their physical training regimes to help them prepare for peak performance, and be ready to perform when it really matters. Football players cannot reproduce in training the intensity of taking the vital kick in a penalty shoot-out in a World Cup Final (as many have found to their cost). However, by visioning, they can play the scene over in their head hundreds of times, and actually create physical changes in their brains. As a result, they possess the neural 'experience' to go along with their football skills that allows them to hold their nerve, blank out the crowd, and do exactly what they have done a hundred times before in their heads.

Muhammad Ali described this best, when he said, "The fight is won or lost far away from witnesses – behind the lines, in the gym, and out there on the road, long before I dance under those lights".

What Ali was describing was what he dubbed 'future history'. He trained his mind for the fight, as well as his body. He mentally rehearsed the fight in his head, over and over again, in the weeks leading up to a bout. In fact, out of the 19 bouts in his professional career, in which Ali made a prediction (e.g. *'Archie Moore, you're going in round four'),* 17 had the outcome exactly as he had stated. It was as if he had rehearsed the fight so many times in his head, that when it came to the real thing, he knew exactly what he was going to do next, right down to finishing the fight off in the round he had visualised in his 'future history'

Steve McDermott, the author of *'How to be a complete and utter failure in life, work and everything' (2002)* [Ref 7], describes the impact of visualisation on Leon Taylor in the run up to the Olympic games in Athens in 2004. Leon was a British 10m diver who had been unable to secure better than fourth place in any major championships. As Athens approached, he started to run 'mind movies' of the full seven days leading up the diving final. He created vivid images of daily activities (training perfectly), how he would be feeling (very confident), how he was sleeping (very comfortably). On the day of the final he spoke about it being like "putting in the DVD and pressing play". He secured an Olympic Silver medal that day, the first British diver in 47 years to win a medal in the sport.

So, why does this work? As mentioned previously, the brain does not differentiate between the thought of an imagined action and a real action, and so is effectively rehearsing and practicing real actions when imagined. Lynne McTaggart, in her book *The Intention Experiment, 2007* [Ref 8], *describes an experiment with a group of skiers who were wired up to an* electromyograph (EMG) device. It was found that when the skiers mentally rehearsed their downhill runs, the electrical impulses sent to the muscles were the same as when they were physically engaged in the runs.

Another extraordinary example of the power of mental imagery is described by **Amy Brann** in her book, *Make Your Brain Work, 2013,* [Ref 9], in which she describes an experiment by *Yeu & Cole,* where imagining you are exercising a muscle can actually strengthen the muscle. One group were provided a simple physical exercise routine to work on a finger daily for four weeks. Another group were provided instructions to simply imagine doing the exercises, together with an 'imaginary' motivating voice shouting at them to contract their finger harder. At the end of the four week period, the physical exercise group had increased their finger strength by 20%, while the 'imagined work' group had increased finger strength of 22%.

And, what might this mean for people in business, and particularly people with leadership responsibility? How much time is spent in your organisation in looking in the rear view mirror.' Think about it! What is the predominant focus of meetings, reviews, reports and so on? Is the focus on what has been going wrong, and why? How much time is devoted to looking at trends, graphs, and budget forecasts based on productivity over the last month, quarter or year? How much of the employee performance appraisal is devoted to the fine detail of relative value and contribution of people over the past quarter or year, and not about the development, potential and possibilities in the future?

When people become obsessed by the problems of the here and now, the next decision, the next quarterly review or the next performance appraisal, they are focusing on the ailment.

Where is the vision in all of this? How is 'future history' being created? Effective leaders constantly scan the horizon, looking beyond today's (and yesterday's!) issues, and mentally rehearse future successes. Truly great leaders are then able to inspire people to share in this vision, so that whole teams, and entire organisations, harness the power of their combined vision and well-rehearsed 'mind movies'.

CHAPTER FOUR KEY LEARNING POINTS

- The Power of Dreams
- Positive Visualisation
- The impact of creating 'Future History'

CHAPTER FOUR REFLECTIONS

What form will 'future history' take for you and your business?

_____

_____

_____

_____

_____

_____

_____

How will you recognise when you are being successful? List a few of the key ways you will know.

_____

_____

_____

_____

_____

_____

_____

What's possible? Allow yourself to dream big and capture what comes to mind.

_____

_____

_____

_____

_____

_____

_____

_____

Chapter Five   The Inner Game

Quietening the inner voice

In July 2012 Andy Murray became the first British men's player to reach the singles final at Wimbledon in 74 years. Although he lost in a great final to an inspired Roger Federer, something happened that day that suggested that Murray had buried a number of ghosts that had been haunting him around the grand slam circuit for several years. In fact, what was most pleasing about Murray's performance in that final, even more than the level of tennis performance that he put in, was the **'Inner Game'** he played.

All sports, games and activities that people undertake can be thought about on two levels. The outer game is the one played out physically, and witnessed by others. In the case of tennis it includes the serves, ground strokes, smashes and lobs. But more often than not, especially in a contest between two players of comparable skill levels, it is the one that plays the better Inner Game who comes through and wins.

The Inner Game is played out completely inside the brain. To succeed, one must quieten the **unhelpful 'voice'** in the head that judges, criticises and worries. It can act in many subtle (and not so subtle) ways, but basically it does one of two things. It either causes us to **dwell on and regret past events** (e.g. a poorly executed drop shot at the end of the last rally that cost you the game), or it worries about and **raises anxiety levels about future events** (e.g. if I don't win my next service game, my opponent will be serving for the match). Neither of these thought processes are useful or conducive to delivering your peak performance. To perform at your best, you need to be operating neither in the past nor in the future, but with **total concentration on the present**.

This applies, of course, not just to tennis, sports or games, but to our everyday lives. Consider just how much of your own thinking time is preoccupied with concerns or regrets about past events or with anxiety about deadlines or future presentations?

Tim Gallwey coined the phrase '*The Inner Game*' in his seminal work, *The Inner Game of Tennis, 1975,* [Ref 2]. Its simple messages about quieting our inner voice, and questioning traditional 'teaching' and 'coaching' methods, are every bit as applicable to how we operate, function and interact in our personal and working lives, as they are to tennis. He uses the following simple formula to describe excellence; **Excellence = Potential minus Interference** (where interference is all of the internal negative thoughts, doubts, limiting beliefs, self-criticism and judgement that we are capable of inflicting on ourselves on a regular basis).

Gallwey also outlines the typical methods of learning that people tend to adopt :-

- **Criticize** or judge past behaviour
- **Tell yourself to change** – with self-talk usually
- **Try hard** – make yourself do it right
- **Critical judgement of results** – leading to repetition of the process

Each and every step of this process moves us further away from concentrating on the present, focusing our attention instead on the unchangeable past and trying to change the future.

Gallwey's Inner Game method of learning offers an alternative approach which helps rid us of all the non-helpful self-talk that interferes with our potential:

- **Observe existing behaviour** (non-judgementally!)
- **Ask yourself to change** – using image and feel – do not try to correct for errors
- **Let it happen**
- **Non-judgemental**, calm observation of results – leading to continuing observation of process until behaviour is automatic

Using this approach, the player (or worker) knows the goal, but is not emotionally involved in achieving it, and instead can watch the results emerge with calmness. This *'just observe it'* approach helps one to concentrate only on what is currently happening, rather than being emotionally distracted by past events or future possibilities.

As we know from the previous chapter, creating 'future history' can also play an enormous part in being successful. So, you might be wondering whether these two approaches, *visualisation and inner game*, are contradictory. I don't believe they are. The benefit of visualising and mentally rehearsing future outcomes is that it actually results in neuronal changes within the brain *(The Brain that Changes Itself, Norman Doidge, 2007)* [Ref 10]. By making the vision created as real and vivid as possible, the brain becomes better prepared to deal with whatever is thrown at it (challenges, setbacks, doubts) when the time arrives, and it finds itself in a 'winning' position. But, having prepared the brain in advance with the vivid images and feelings of winning, when you are in the thick of the action, it is important to focus on the here and now, and not be distracted by conscious thoughts of crossing the line. This makes sense when you think of when you are at your best in business. Having a clear sense of purpose and direction is vital to give you the drive and motivation for making good decisions, but when deeply absorbed in an intense or challenging situation, such as a negotiation or a performance discussion, having absolute focus on what is going on in the room, actively listening and being completely present is paramount to you being as effective as you can be. If you have done your 'homework' and created those 'brain changing' images, they will help guide your decisions at a sub-conscious level.

So why is all this relevant to Andy Murray losing at Wimbledon? Well, for those of you who watched that emotionally charged final, his tearful speech in front of a packed Centre Court and millions more on TV was hard to watch. But, despite the despair and pain that he (and his followers) felt, it was clear that something had changed. His raw talent was clearly good enough to win the major prizes. His tactical awareness was not in question. His physical fitness had been transformed such that no-one in the game worked harder to ensure they were able to go the distance. The final piece of the jigsaw for Andy was clearly conquering his *Inner Game*. For years his temperament had been called into question. He cracked at the big moments. The pressure placed on him by the British media and public, hungry for a British Wimbledon men's champion, was becoming unbearable. If Andy was to succeed, it was going to be a victory inside his own head that would secure the breakthrough.

On that Sunday in July 2012, as Andy let his emotions loose in public, something had clearly changed, and two massive opportunities, in the shape of the Olympics and the US Open, presented themselves within the following two months to prove that it had. Murray was about to go in to those as a changed person, with a new game playing out inside his head. And, he indeed took both of those tournaments by storm.

On the same Centre Court at Wimbledon that had been the site of such pain, just 28 days previously, he swept to Olympic Gold, by beating his great rival Novak Djokovic in the semi-final, and the undisputed king of Wimbledon's Centre Court, Roger Federer, in an amazingly one-sided final. He had certainly buried some ghosts, but winning a slam was still how he would be judged. One month later, at Flushing Meadow, New York, he made his biggest breakthrough yet. He out-played, out-thought and out-slogged Djokovic, in a nail-biting US Open final, and his place in tennis grand slam history was now secured.

Wind forward one year to July 2013, and we find ourselves back at Wimbledon. Despite all his success, there is still a monkey on Murray's back. Wimbledon is the pinnacle, particularly for a British tennis player, especially given the 77 years since Fred Perry last won it as a home-based player. He is reminded of this fact every time he is interviewed or opens a newspaper. What a difference a year makes. No-one would have taken a bet one year previously on Murray beating Djokovic in three straight sets. Probably not even Murray himself. He wouldn't have had the belief, or the *Inner Game* to do what he did in the 2013 final. His resilience, his focus, his temperament, and his absolute unwavering belief were astounding to watch.

> CHAPTER FIVE KEY LEARNING POINTS
>
> - Master 'the inner game'
> - Eliminate internal interference
> - Focus on the present
> - Let it happen (without judgement)

CHAPTER FIVE REFLECTIONS

What things are contributing to the 'interference' that is taking away from your potential, and reducing your effectiveness? What about in your teams, and across your company?

_____

_____

_____

_____

_____

_____

How much attention is being diverted away from the present and being wasted on regret about the past or anxiety about the future? Capture any examples that come to mind where this is happening.

_____

_____

_____

_____

_____

_____

_____

What is possible for you and your business if the *inner game* can be mastered allowing you to be completely present? Remove all constraints from your mind and imagine complete mastery.

_____

_____

_____

_____

_____

_____

Chapter Six   Playing the 'A' Game

Golfing Interference

I was intrigued by something that Rory McIlroy said in an interview in March 2013, following his widely-reported 'early exit' from the Honda Golf Classic in Florida. The young golfer, from Holywood, Northern Ireland, had become the new superstar of that sport in the previous 12 months, rocketing to number one in the world in the process. It was clear in early 2013, however, that he was going through a troubled time, with speculation bouncing between whether it was down to his new club sponsorship deal, his relationship with tennis star Caroline Wozniaki, or, as he claimed during the tournament in Florida, a troublesome wisdom tooth.

McIlroy described how he feels when he is off his game in very simple terms. "I always think when I'm playing bad that it's further away than it is." (meaning his best game). I suspect this is true for many of us, in all walks of life. Rory went on to say "… If I have a bad round, it's sort of like the end of the world."

This 'catastrophizing' form of thinking is, I am sure, familiar to many of us. When some aspect of our life (not necessarily one that is most critical) is not working as well as we'd like, it can become magnified and generalised, to the extent that it contaminates our thinking and self-perception of other aspects of what we do and who we are.

Later in the interview, I was impressed with the realization that Rory had come to (no doubt with the aid of his psychologist or coach), that playing badly does not necessarily mean that his 'A-game' is a long way off. In fact, it is often the case that what we want is much nearer than we imagine.

I have seen this same breakthrough in thinking arise during coaching sessions. Clients can sometimes struggle to get to grips with describing or imagining their vision. They start out thinking a vision must be able to be described in terms of a place, or a point in time *(usually a relatively long way off)*, and often with trappings *(typically materialistic in nature)*. After exploring this from different directions for a while, what often emerges as a huge breakthrough, and indeed a relief, is when people experience a shift in thinking that allows them to see their vision as being a 'state of mind', a way of thinking, and, often, a state that is not necessarily so far away.

Like Rory, the breakthrough happens first inside our heads, not out on the golf course, or in our working environments. Once we resolve this, our best game is ready and waiting to be played.

Yet another area where mental interference shows up in sport, and in particular in the world of golf, is with the notorious 'Yips'. The yips is a well-known phenomenon and a curse to golfers. It is whispered about quietly in golf club corridors for fear that the very word being spoken might afflict those within earshot. A number of golfers, who have had successful careers, whether as professionals or top-level amateurs, report a number of strange feelings when they are poised over even the simplest of putts. They may freeze and cannot release the club to strike the ball. Or they may start their backswing and twitch or jerk just before impact resulting in dramatic over or under-strikes.

But, what is actually going on? Well, it can be described as involuntary muscle contractions which prevent people from carrying out a particular physical movement smoothly. It dramatically interferes with fine motor skills associated with putting in golf, as well as in other sports requiring similar motor skills, such as snooker, darts and bowling in cricket.

As we have seen in the previous chapter, the inner game is won when the inner critic is silenced, allowing you to focus in a clear, calm way on the present. Interference from worrying about past mistakes, or over-thinking the outcome, inevitably degrades performance. When a player feels under pressure, perhaps as a result of having played a series of bad strokes, one strategy the mind can adopt is to start over-analysing the mechanics of the problem. "Am I gripping the club too tight?" "Too loose?" "Is my stance correct?" "Perhaps I need to make a slight adjustment of my wrists?" This becomes a dangerous spiral, particularly in the middle of a game. It is usually associated with a rising emotional reaction, all of which is guaranteed to take us away from the very state of inner calm that we know is required to produce our best results.

Shane Warne, the legendary Australian cricketer, has shared some of his tips to avoid succumbing to the yips. (*The Sporting Edge*) [Ref 11].

- **Play to enjoy the sport** and don't let the inner critic or over-analysis ruin your day.
- **Create psychological 'routines'** between balls (or between shots in the case of golf) to manage thinking and performance – and help you stay present
- **Practice with a tune** (or other 'ritual') in your head when under pressure – it stops you over-thinking
- **Setbacks are more about character than sport** Feel your confidence grow as you tackle your fears.

Our best performances, whether in sport or in business, are often played instinctively, when we are deeply immersed in the moment. We work out our strategy and game plan before we step out into the arena, but once we are in the thick of the action, we are at our best when we commit 100%, with a clear and focused mind, to the next action, trusting that our homework has been done, and that we will make the right decisions. When all this comes together, whether in sport or business, people experience the game or task as simple and enjoyable, conditions that help them deliver their A-game.

> CHAPTER SIX KEY LEARNING POINTS
>
> - Your 'A-game' is closer than you think
> - Vision as a 'state of mind'
> - Quieten the 'inner critic'
> - Create familiar routines to stay present

CHAPTER SIX REFLECTIONS

Are you delivering your 'A' game, day in and day out? If not, list some scenarios where you would like to be?

_____

_____

_____

_____

_____

_____

_____

If not, what's preventing you from doing so? Write down the things you are saying to yourself that are getting in your way?

_____

_____

_____

_____

_____

_____

_____

What about other people in your business?   What could people be doing better on a regular basis?

_____

_____

_____

_____

_____

_____

_____

When things go badly, what are your typical 'go to' responses?

Do you have any rituals to help you remain focused on the present and quieten the inner critic? What are they? Or, what might they be?

___

___

___

___

___

___

Chapter Seven — Optimists Win

Bouncing back from disappointment

A great deal of pressure was heaped on the young shoulders of Matt Biondi in the run up to the Seoul Olympics in 1988. He was one of the United States great hopes for multiple medals in the swimming pool. Comparisons were being drawn with the legendary Mark Spitz who had won seven golds in the 1972 games. In his first event, the two-hundred-metre freestyle, he finished a creditable third. Great by most people's standards, but disappointing for Biondi and the hard-to-please media back home. The next event was the one-hundred-metre butterfly. Having blasted into an early lead, and dominated the race all the way, he made an error of judgement on his final stroke. One more stroke squeezed in with a metre to go would have seen him home, but he chose to coast and stretch for the wall instead. In doing so he was pipped by a fingernail and beaten into second by an unknown swimmer, Anthony Nesty, from Surinam, not a country renowned for swimmers, let alone gold medals.

There was much gnashing of teeth and criticism levelled at Biondi from afar. This was not the start to an assault on seven gold medals that the American public expected, and many started to write him off. There was at least one person who did not, however. Marty Seligman, the father of Positive Psychology, watching proceedings on his television, had belief, and evidence, that Biondi had what it would take to come back from these disappointments and go on to achieve success. Seligman had run an assessment programme with the U.S. women and men's swimming team in the run up to the Olympics that year [Ref 12]. The objective was to assess how each of the squad would perform, especially when under pressure and after setbacks. Having tested and assigned each swimmer on an optimism vs pessimism scale, as well as on their explanatory style (i.e. the reasons people give for things going wrong), Seligman then created a set of circumstances which simulated defeat for the swimmers during the course of their training. Each swimmer was asked to put in one of their biggest efforts on their best event. They were timed by their coach (who was, of course, in on the experiment). On completion, the swimmer was then told that their time was worse than the actual time they had achieved. Now, elite swimmers are highly attuned to their timings, and can normally estimate fairly accurately what they have achieved. The level of the 'failure' was made sufficiently large to be very disappointing, but not so large as to be obviously wrong. After a rest period, and some time to absorb the disappointment, the swimmers were asked to do the same event again, as fast as they could.

There was a marked difference between optimists and pessimists in their reactions to the 'failure' and, more importantly, in how they performed in their repeat swim. Seligman observed that one swimmer, assessed as a pessimist, "sat and rocked like a baby in a corner for twenty minutes afterwards". Once rested and refocused, and back in the pool, pessimists performed worse. Their times deteriorated, even lower than their 'correct' first swim, some by as much as two seconds, the difference between coming first and last in those events. Optimists, on the other hand, either sustained their performance, at least as good as they had swum the first time, or, in some cases, they went even faster. Matt Biondi had been one of those who responded to the disappointment by getting even faster.

This is why Marty Seligman was confident he would bounce back from those first two events in Seoul, and he did just that. Biondi went on to repay Seligman's confidence by winning all of his next five events, securing five golds to go along with his silver and bronze.

Seligman is one of the great names in modern psychology, and is credited with changing the direction of thinking within the field, with his ground-breaking work on learned helplessness, depression and optimism [Ref 12]. As well as the work done with the Olympic swimmers, he has also undertaken detailed analysis of baseball and basketball teams. He painstakingly reviewed all interviews, comments and sound-bites given by players and coaches from certain teams over entire seasons and assessed them according to what he describes as 'explanatory style'. Explanatory style is key in Seligman's view, as it predicts so much about how a person will respond to setbacks, failures and disappointments.

The key appears to be to what extent people attribute failure to something permanent, how pervasive it is deemed to be, and whether the reason is felt to be internal or down to something external.

Let's take a look at how some of the baseball players and coaches explained defeats. For one team, the New York Mets, in the 1985 season, responses along the following lines were typical:

- **"We lost because they made the play tonight."**
- **"It must have been one of those days."**
- **"He (the opponent) hit well tonight."**
- **"It wasn't my day."**
- **"Some moisture must have gotten on the ball."**

So, when the Mets did badly, the pattern of responses that their players made fell into a consistent pattern. The reasons were typically *non-permanent* (e.g. it's just for today), *non-pervasive* (e.g. it doesn't happen against everyone we play – it was just these opponents), and *external* (e.g. it was not our fault, something outside our control happened).

Contrast this with responses given by the St. Louis Cardinals in the same season:

- "We can't hit. What the Hell, let's face it."
- "It's a mental thing. We were too relaxed."
- "I don't have the expertise."
- "It was a real catchable ball. I just didn't catch it."
- "I am having a lot of trouble concentrating and keeping my mind on the job."

A very different set of responses, I'm sure you will agree. These explanations certainly do suggest that the coaches and players see the issues as *permanent* (e.g. we can't hit), *pervasive* (e.g. I don't have the expertise) and *internal* (e.g. trouble concentrating).

The interesting part of this study happened the following season. Both the Mets and Cardinals had disappointing seasons in 1985, the Cardinals just missing out by the narrowest of margins in the World Series to Kansas. Despite the Cardinals having a more talented team than the Mets (as generally accepted by expert judges in these matters and backed up by all the statistical averages), the Mets bounced back to outperform the Cardinals in the 1986 season, reaching and winning the World Series. The Cardinals collapsed and finished nowhere. This relative difference in performance was what Seligman predicted based on the analysis he carried out in the previous year.

Seligman's conviction that optimism, coupled with appropriate explanatory styles, as a huge predictor of success was not confined to the sports field, however. He took his theory into the board room of one of the world's largest insurance companies, Met Life. In the mid-1980s, the newly appointed head of Met Life had been wrestling with a problem that was shared with all other insurance companies. Identifying and retaining the best and most talented people to do the extremely difficult job of selling life insurance.

The industry as a whole had been hiring tens of thousands of new agents every year. Even after careful selection, screening, interviewing and training, half of them quit in the first year, and by the end of the fourth year, eighty percent had disappeared. Just as worrying, those that remained became less and less productive. It was costing Met Life seventy-five million dollars in hiring costs alone each year. Seligman was set the challenge of working out whether he could do a better job of predicting who would succeed and who would not, and, in the process, improve the selection process for Met Life.

The task of selling life insurance in the 1980s was, and I dare say still is, challenging. It is well accepted that most calls will result in rejection. Only those agents who persist, and are not dispirited by rejection, will eventually make the call that results in an appointment and eventually a sale. Once again, as in the swimming and baseball scenarios, it was the explanatory style of the agents that was to determine who would succeed and who would quit. Given that most calls result in a response such as, "No, I'm not interested", or perhaps even something more abusive, it is worth looking at what typical agent reactions to these outcomes look like.

Pessimistic agents typically say things to themselves that have the hallmarks of being permanent, pervasive and internal, such as:

- "I'm no good."
- "No one wants to buy insurance from me."
- "I can't even get past the first call."

Agents with an optimistic approach are more likely to explain rejections in the following types of way:

- "He was obviously too busy right now."
- "They probably already have insurance."
- "I called during supper."

While the pessimist will find making the next call after rejection (and their self-talk) harder to do, the optimist will plough on to the next call and eventually achieve an appointment or sale quicker and with less internal turmoil than the pessimist.

Seligman introduced a new selection method for Met Life, based on explanatory style. Using this method, a 'special' cadre of agents were hired (who under previous selection methods would have been rejected), all of whom scored high on explanatory style, and were monitored for the next two years. This group outsold regularly recruited pessimists by 57 percent after two years, and even outsold the average of the regular recruits by 27 percent. The key quality that Seligman's test appeared to be tapping into was persistence. Talent and motivation are clearly important in any walk of life, but persistence in the face of constant rejection and disappointment is a factor that appears to be a greater predictor of success.

Met Life went on to adopt the explanatory style selection method, helping it to reject candidates that it would previously have brought into the company (many of whom they would presumably have lost soon after). In addition they recruited people who would otherwise have been rejected using traditional selection methods, an approach which has helped turn round Met Life's fortunes within this hugely competitive industry.

Cold-calling type jobs may be unique in terms of the level of direct rejection that people can expect to face on a daily basis, but all jobs, in all sectors, at all levels, are littered with a whole range of setbacks, obstacles, difficulties, challenges and failures. These will come in many different guises; some may be technical in nature, some inter-personal, some perhaps even dangerous. In all cases, optimists, with explanatory styles that focus on the reasons for setbacks being temporary, specific and external, are best equipped to 'bounce-back' and succeed in the long term.

If you are in the business of recruiting, and you are faced with two people of equivalent talent and can only recruit one, Seligman would argue you should recruit the more optimistic of the two.

If you are seeking to form a team from people already in your company, give some thought to the roles you place people in based on optimism and pessimism. Pessimists can be extremely effective when things are going well, but be cautious about how you use them soon after a disappointment. They may require a period of building up again, away from the action.

And don't give up on pessimists. They can be trained to become optimists, or at least pessimists with more effective explanatory styles.

CHAPTER SEVEN KEY LEARNING POINTS

- Optimism wins out over pessimism
- Treat setbacks as temporary not permanent
- Think of failures as specific and not pervasive

CHAPTER SEVEN REFLECTIONS

What is the pre-dominant explanatory style within your organisation? What sort of comments do you hear in response to failures?

_____

_____

_____

_____

_____

_____

How well do you and your teams respond to setbacks and failures? What areas for improvement can you identify?

The Vital Edge

What more might be possible for your company if it could have a more optimistic outlook and a more positive explanatory style? In what ways could this be achieved?

_____

_____

_____

_____

_____

_____

_____

The Vital Edge

PART III   MOTIVATION

Let's now look at the key role played by motivation in determining performance.   Motivation has a long and interesting history in the story of psychological research and theories of performance. It has been the cornerstone of much of the principles upon which business structures have been built since the industrial revolution. The science of management at that time was mainly concerned with how to improve productivity in an environment that was increasingly becoming task-based and production line driven. As such, the focus was almost exclusively on incentivisation. 'Carrot and stick' became the overwhelming tool of management to drive workers to produce more in less time.

Other enlightened thinkers knew, of course, that there was much more to human motivation than the over-simplistic external reward and punishment spectrum. There was something very important about people's intrinsic (or internal) motivation, which was, at that time being largely ignored.

Sport, once again, provides us with a fascinating glimpse into the world of the athlete, and allows us to hold up a mirror to ourselves and our business cultures, and to ask some challenging questions about whether the motivational balance is right in our lives and organisations.

Chapter Eight   Breaking Barriers

The 4-minute mile

While watching the Olympic Games from London in 2012, it was remarkable to watch records tumble and barriers being broken on a daily basis. Of course, not all barriers are measured by distance or by the clock. Some of the most fascinating are psychological barriers.

Andy Murray, as we saw in in chapter 5, appeared to have broken through a personal barrier in winning his Olympic singles gold medal, followed by the US Open and Wimbledon. Michael Phelps broke the barrier of all-time most decorated Olympian – 22 medals – 18 of which are gold. This is a phenomenal achievement, even in a sport that provides more opportunity than most to 'multi-event'. Phelps has set the bar at a new height for someone else to emulate in years to come.

Some barriers are broken with increasing regularity, most notably in the swimming pool and in the velodrome, the latter no doubt assisted by advances in cycle technology. Others stand defiantly unobtainable, such as the long jump record which has stood for over 20 years. But, it is the psychological nature of breaking barriers that is always the most fascinating.

Perhaps the best known example of a psychological barrier in the world of athletics, is that of the 4-minute mile. Until 1954, many actually believed that it was impossible, dangerous, and perhaps even fatal, for anyone to run a mile faster than 4 mins. Roger Bannister became the first to make the breakthrough, and opened the floodgates for many others to do the same very soon afterwards. Soon the record was being broken over and over again. Those people who were soon running sub-4 minutes on a regular basis were clearly physically capable of doing so, in the same way that Bannister did. The barrier they broke was inside their head, not on the track.

Running the 100m had a similar 'magical' barrier for quite some time. Once 10 sec was broken by Jim Hines in 1968, many others soon followed. The 100m final at the 2012 Olympics was won by the extraordinary Usain Bolt. Had Asafa Powell not pulled up with an injury, there is no doubt that every one of the finalists in the race would have gone under 10sec.

No-one has yet gone under 2 hours for the marathon, but it is getting closer, with the current world record for men standing at 2hr 03min. It will be fascinating to observe how long it takes for the first person to run 1hr 59min 59sec, and how long afterwards we have to wait to see that time further reduced.

What is going on with these 'symbolic barriers', and what learning can it provide for other areas of life? In business, when people say "it's impossible," do they simply mean "it's not been done yet"? Does it mean that they are not prepared to put the effort in to make it possible? Or, do they just need someone else to do it first, to prove it can be done, before they follow?

How can leaders take this phenomenon in sport and use it to inspire people to break through barriers? How can leaders point the way and help people to see that with the correct focus, teamwork, application and commitment, barriers need not be insurmountable; that barriers are not the end of the line, but just another staging post on a longer journey.

What are some of the learning points leaders and people in business can take from sport and high performance athletes?

Pressure Pressure to top athletes is viewed as a privilege. Michael Johnson, the 400m world record holder, describes the pressure he felt in this way. It was what he was in the top tier for, to compete against and beat the best, and if he wasn't feeling pressure something was wrong. The key here has to be about how to view the pressure – to see it as a source of energy, an aid to focusing on the task at hand, and not as a force that causes you to freeze, or be afraid of what lies ahead.

Teamwork   The importance of team is paramount (as we have explored in the earlier chapters of this book), and even in the most individual and lonely of sports, the top performers are always quick to recognise that their success only comes as a result of a huge team effort – coaches, physios, dieticians, training partners, family, and so on. No one achieves greatness alone. Trust of others in the team to do their part is essential. Cycling and rowing have demonstrated that it is the team who works together, who have a plan and a rhythm that is executed excellently that wins, not necessarily the best individuals. This is a huge piece of learning, as so much more can be achieved this way, more than any one individual is capable of.

Learning   Continual learning and a hunger for knowledge mark out high performers. Feedback on performance – particularly where things did not go to plan, and when some may label it failure – are sources of huge potential learning. Too often in business, performance management and constructive feedback can turn in to a 'battleground' where little value is created. Seeking new techniques and looking to see what others are doing is essential in sport, and in business. Innovation and creativity are vital to keep moving forward and in finding that winning edge. **Marginal gains (to be discussed in detail in chapter 13)** depend on creativity, which requires being open to learning. Sir Clive Woodward, British Olympic Association's Director of Elite Performance, looks for 'teachability' when assessing young prospective talent (see chapter 11). A thirst for knowledge, the desire to learn, and becoming expert in their chosen sport are all signs that tell Sir Clive so much more than simply the physical attributes and raw talent of the young athlete.

Demonstrate the art of the possible   Leaders play a vital role in coaching people. Coaching is a hugely powerful process for removing demons, doubts and concerns, and helping people to become aware of their own limiting beliefs. Leaders as role models are able to inspire and motivate, opening doors to allow others to charge through.

Resilience   Athletes suffer setbacks and many describe their journeys as being more occupied with downs than ups. They experience many failures, injuries and defeats, but it is the building of resilience that sees them succeed. Staying focused on the big vision or prize is an essential quality to survive in the tough world of sport, but equally in the world of business.

Above all, the ability to not see barriers as obstacles, but merely as temporary staging posts on a journey that continues on the other side, is a vital mindset to adopt in both sport and in business.

CHAPTER EIGHT KEY LEARNING POINTS

- Psychological barriers
- How are barriers or 'stages' viewed?
- Pressure and its role in performance
- The importance of role modelling
- Resilience and how it can be developed

CHAPTER EIGHT REFLECTIONS

How do you and your team view challenges that have not been achieved before? Capture some examples you or your team have faced.

_____

_____

_____

_____

_____

_____

_____

Is it easier to tread the paths that are well-worn, or do you regularly push out into territory that has not been explored? Give examples where you have done. If not, capture examples where you would have liked to have done this.

_____

_____

_____

_____

_____

_____

_____

How are setbacks and disappointments managed within your organisation? As failures, or as opportunities for learning? Recall and capture some examples of each.

_____

_____

_____

_____

_____

_____

Chapter Nine   Motivation

The dual-sport Olympic champion

We explored in previous sections the importance of the 'inner game' in producing effective performance, but how significant is the role of external motivation?

Although the initial motivation for most people to engage in a sport or activity is typically due to some 'internal' drive, such as seeking fun, pleasure, excitement or a search for self-worth, the role of 'external' factors in helping keep people motivated and striving to keep improving should not be underestimated.

Reflecting on the extraordinary performances of the world's top sprinters, it is clear that they benefit from having strong competition to challenge them. On some occasions this can be achieved by colleagues within the same team pushing each other to ever-higher levels, as evidenced by the Jamaican sprinters, Usain Bolt and Yohan Blake. It may also be achieved by fierce but respectful rivalry between opponents, where the standards of excellence set by one player forces the other to have to raise their game to heights they would not otherwise have reached.

Likewise, in the world of tennis, the phenomenal standard of performance displayed by the world's top players in the last decade is evidence of this. It is inconceivable that Rafael Nadal would ever have reached such performance levels had he not been asked some extraordinary questions on the tennis court by Roger Federer. In a similar way, Novak Djokovic has since taken his game to even greater heights to become World Number One. Previously a clay court specialist, Nadal has since worked even harder to adapt his game so that he is capable of winning on any surface. In 2013, he returned from a serious knee injury, followed by intense training and conditioning, to recapture the number one spot once again, having taken his game to an even higher level. Most tennis fans would argue that this current era of men's tennis, dominated by Federer, Djokovic and Nadal, has been one of the richest in the history of the sport. But, it is unlikely that the standard of tennis we have seen from this trio would ever have reached such amazing levels had they not all emerged on the scene together. Put simply, in order to beat each other they have had to become increasingly more accomplished in their performance.

Competition is just one of a number of external motivators that is capable of eliciting higher levels of performance. Other forms of external motivation may also be important for some people.

Reward & Reinforcement Given the astronomical sums of money that are paid to the top sports stars around the world, it is easy to slip into thinking that this is one of the major reasons why people play sport. Of course, the rewards may help motivate some people to stay in the sport, or to improve, but it is unlikely to be the reason they took up the sport in the first place. If anything, the financial rewards will be icing on the cake for already successful athletes. In fact, if athletes are predominantly motivated by such external factors as money, then they are more likely to suffer from dips in performance as a result of becoming discouraged when things don't go well. People who are driven more by internal factors, and treat financial rewards as a 'bonus' for doing something they love, are much more likely to have the resilience and desire to work through those periods, placing less pressure on themselves in the process *(Inside Sport Psychology, C.I. Karageorghis and P.C. Terry, 2011)* [Ref 13].

Retaining enjoyment and fun for years is often a challenge for top sports people. They can lose contact with what it was that made them take up the sport and love it so much in the first place. It too often becomes about the next contract, dealing with the press, pressure of keeping their place in the team, or the pressure of winning medals. They stop enjoying the sport, and some even walk away to seek other ways to find internal satisfaction. Those that play on solely for the purpose of gaining externally generated satisfaction and rewards (e.g. money or adulation) rarely experience extended careers at the top.

Recognition & Leaving a Legacy   For some people, being recognised as being successful is a powerful driver. Winning medals, crowd adulation or favourable press write-ups are, for these people, more significant motivators than money. The case of Rebecca Romero demonstrates this most powerfully. Rebecca is a truly unique Olympian in that she won a silver medal as a rower in the Beijing Olympics in 2008, and four years later in London achieved gold in a totally different sport, cycling. Her remarkable story and overwhelming desire to achieve gold is taken up by Chris Boardman (the former Olympic pursuit champion), who was a technical adviser to the British cycling team in the lead up to 2012. He said that, "It was her absolute need to win a gold medal and her commitment to the process that stood out". Her obsession with winning gold at times threatened to overwhelm her, and her coaches did have to, at times, save her from herself by taking her out of training to stop her burning out, such was her desire to reach perfection. Romero was later to say, "Becoming an Olympic champion, to have medals in two sports, I'm so proud of myself. I was never really good at sports. I never really thought I was good at riding bikes. It's just hard work. I wanted a gold. I wanted to be a champion. Now I've put down my mark to be remembered." (BBC Olympic Blog) [Ref 14].

Being part of a team For others it is important that whatever they achieve they do it as part of a team. The camaraderie and support associated with working together to achieve success and being part of a successful group is a powerful motivator in its own right.

Peer pressure   A less constructive, but nevertheless powerful, group-inspired motivation can be generated by peer pressure. This may show up as people wanting to keep up with colleagues to avoid losing face, being embarrassed or being outdone.

But it is not only sports performance that can benefit from external motivation. Channelled effectively, using rivalry and competition, or people's desire for recognition or legacy, can be hugely important in driving up standards in all walks of life. It is vital, however, that internal and external motivation are carefully balanced, and leaders need to be aware of the pit-falls of placing all or too much emphasis on attempting to drive increased performance with external motivators.

As will be discussed in more depth shortly in Chapter 10, 'Flow' is a hugely desirable state, associated with total immersion in a task and 'peak performance'. It is also associated with and based upon a building block of internal motivation. In an ideal world, achieving a flow state would rely exclusively on internal factors like internally generated reward and reinforcement and becoming completely immersed in the task, often described as being 'in the zone'. In this ideal world, a workforce 'in flow' will be operating at peak performance and need no external motivation to stay there. Of course, in the real world, the likelihood is that both will be important, with a strong emphasis on having as strong and wide a foundation as possible based on internal motivation, and the external used as a secondary level of motivation.

A classic illustration of the dangers of believing that you can use external motivators, like rewards, to improve people's performance on any task is outlined powerfully by Dan Pink *(see his excellent 2009 TED talk on the Puzzle of Motivation)* [Ref 15].

In fact, Pink goes so far as to say that business is ignoring the science, and that the wrong behaviours are being rewarded if we are to succeed in changing and improving the performance of business employees. Most problems and challenges our big businesses and organisations face today cannot be solved with the old 'industrial factory' way of doing things. Companies, organisations and governments are looking for creative, innovative solutions to intangible and intellectual problems. Despite this, society in general is reluctant to break away from the traditional factory model that links reward with motivation.

The evidence is clear. Stretch goals and offering people bigger rewards to solve intellectual problems actually has the effect of lowering performance. It is, in fact, a disincentive. Bonuses work well only in cases of clear, well-defined and narrowly focused tasks, but, in the case of complex, intellectual problems they actually dull thinking, and cause people to adopt too narrow a focus.

Within a factory-based model of production, when tasks were well-defined and output easily measured, targets, and especially stretch targets, were useful ways to drive up productivity. After all, if you wanted to increase widget production by 10%, you worked people harder, increased the speed of the conveyor, offered bonus targets (or overtime payment), and measured the success of your intervention immediately and directly.

However, most problems and challenges we face today are not of this order. We don't even know the right question in many cases, yet we reward people for achieving stretch goals that produce answers that may not even be correct or appropriate. Despite this, many businesses appear reluctant to break away from the traditional factory model of reward and motivation.

The entire concept is flawed. The incentives system is allegedly "designed to sharpen thinking and accelerate creativity, and it does just the opposite. It dulls thinking and blocks creativity." (Dan Pink)

But, let's be clear. I am not saying that having aspiration and stretching goals or targets is a bad thing. Of course not. Shooting for the stars and seeking to stretch beyond 'normal limits' is what fuels our sportspeople to break records and win golds, and it is what drives our businesses and organisations to make breakthroughs and innovate.

What *is* flawed is attempting to generate discoveries and breakthroughs to complex intellectual problems by using a reward and incentives system based on a 'production line' mind-set.

The greatest sporting achievements on the planet are driven by a complex mix of internal motivation, needs and drives, supplemented by competition, recognition, legacy desires and other social factors such as shared learning, shared achievement and, of course, mastery and 'flow'.

It is time for our business leaders to take the courageous step of turning the traditional performance and reward model on its head, by recognising that simply setting people stretch goals is not the best way to generate the major breakthroughs their companies desire. The science is clear. It is time for our leaders to stop ignoring the evidence. Our collective brain-power and ingenuity needs to be unleashed and not suppressed by out-dated thinking.

CHAPTER NINE KEY LEARNING POINTS

- Differences between Internal & External Motivation
- Competition
- Reward & Reinforcement
- Recognition & Legacy
- Peer Pressure

CHAPTER NINE REFLECTIONS

What does your business believe is the best way to get the best from its people?   List some of the ways that come to mind first.

_____

_____

_____

_____

_____

_____

Is the reward system fit for purpose for the kind of breakthroughs and thinking desired? If not, capture some of the ways that you would like to reform it.

_____

_____

_____

_____

_____

_____

_____

_____

To what extent are differences in what motivates and drives people recognised in your organisation or workplace?

_____

_____

_____

_____

_____

_____

_____

Chapter Ten   In the Flow

Shooting the Rapids

We have all experienced at times, whether you think about sport, business, leisure or recreation, that feeling of being in total control of what you are doing. Sometimes, that feeling can swell to one of exhilaration and complete contentment, where everything you do seems to be effortless and provides a deep sense of enjoyment. It is also associated with internal motivation at its most powerful.

This state is often referred to as 'Flow'. A state of *optimal experience,* so wonderfully examined by Mihaly Csikszentmihalyi in his seminal work, *Flow (The classic book on how to achieve happiness), 1992.* [Ref 26]

Experiences of flow can be found in any walk of life, and not only in extreme situations which stretch the boundaries of human endurance. Some have spoken of the feeling in the midst of horrific situations, such as being imprisoned in a concentration camp, when sharing a crust of bread with a fellow prisoner, or mentally rehearsing a beautiful passage of music. Some people working in factories on monotonous, repetitive, production-line jobs have found ways to challenge themselves by setting small targets and goals in order to create focus and overcome boredom. People who do this report feelings of being in flow. In sport, examples are widespread. Even as a fairly basic level tennis player, I have experienced times when the ball and racquet appear to take on enhanced proportions, time seems to slow down, you anticipate returns from your opponent, and it just feels like you cannot miss the shot.

The aspect of the flow-model that resonated most with me was captured by the importance of being able to attain an optimal balance between current ability (or skill level) and level of challenge on the given task. In simple terms, if you undertake a task that falls far short of the level of ability you currently possess, you are unlikely to be stretched or challenged and the task will pretty soon lead to a state of boredom. Not only that, this is a state where you are unlikely to advance your learning or be motivated to improve your skill. On the other hand, if the level of the challenge presented is far too high for your current level of skill or ability, then the state most likely to be experienced will be one of anxiety, once again, a state that is not conducive to learning or improvement. Under conditions of either boredom or anxiety, it is likely that you will rely more heavily on external motivating factors to keep you going (e.g. the promise of rewards on completion of the task, or unwelcome punishments for failure to complete successfully).

The ideal balance is to be challenged at just about (or actually slightly above) the current level of your ability. Just enough to ensure you are learning and improving, being challenged without becoming anxious, and at a level that maintains concentration and attention, and does not allow a dip down into a state of boredom. Of course, as someone's performance level does increase, the skill-challenge balance at which the flow channel is achieved is going to move too.

This sense of what it means to be in the flow, quite literally, is captured excellently by Haley Daniels, a Canadian national canoeing champion, as she describes handling exceptional conditions at Gull River, Ontario, in the national trials in May 2013 *(National Team Trials Blog, May 2013)* [Ref 16].

The river was in full flood due to very heavy rainfall, making normally challenging rapids even more treacherous, with huge torrents and complex underwater hydraulics. Haley, an experienced canoeist, admits to being intimidated by the conditions, but knew that, more than ever, she had to get herself mentally prepared to take on the conditions. She had invested heavily in mental training to ensure she was able to overcome her fears, and allow her to focus on what she needed to do in the middle of the course. Despite having been disturbed by nightmares of being consumed by roaring rapids, she was highly motivated from within to do her best, and on the day she was able to compose herself, gather her mental strength, and find the 'racing line' in the midst of the torrent of white water. She nailed the race, was placed first in her class, and was selected for the elite Canadian national team as a result.

Where do you find yourself most often as you wend your way on life's journey? Are you firmly in the midst of the river, motivated from within, going with the flow, navigating the hazards and enjoying the thrill of the ride? Or are you bumping along the banks, stopping regularly to re-appraise the situation, before venturing tentatively back in to the turbulent currents in mid-stream.

This river metaphor is very useful, and works on many different levels. I recall listening to **Dan Siegel** (*the eminent neurobiologist and author of Mindsight, The New Science of Personal Transformation, 2010)* [Ref 17], discuss the nature of the mind. He spoke about the healthy mind as being integrated and harmonious ('in flow'), and characterised the troubled mind as tending toward being either 'chaotic' or 'rigid' in manifestation. He refers to these two states as being like opposite banks of a river. When we drop out of flow – *the balanced state of coping, experiencing well-being, and functioning optimally* – we tend to drift toward one or other bank. Which bank you end up on will depend on the condition and situation being experienced, but people do tend to have a dominant bank they typically gravitate toward.

For example, when someone experiences high levels of anxiety or stress, brought on by a particularly challenging business situation (e.g. a bid deadline, a difficult board presentation, or having to resolve conflict in the workplace) they may move toward the 'chaos bank':

On the chaos bank they are likely to resort to behaviours and coping mechanisms that see them work themselves (and others around them) to a frenzy, become ever more demanding, display irritation, have a short fuse and so on.

Others, whose preference is to veer toward the 'rigid bank', tend to respond in a very different way. They are more likely to withdraw, become more isolated, worry in silence, become less vocal, drift into the background at meetings, perhaps even find excuses not to attend, or take time off sick (genuinely or otherwise).

The emotions and behaviours characterised by both of these banks will, in time, create disharmony (both internally for the individual as well as in relation to others), result in relationship breakdown, and take their toll in terms of personal health.

Which bank is chosen is driven largely by our fight-or-flight response, and controlled by the limbic system (the old part of our brain and the seat of our emotions).   Some people may consistently veer toward one or other bank in any number of challenging situations (e.g. stress, rejection, conflict, anxiety), while others may bounce around, swinging between banks depending on problems and difficulties encountered.

During turbulent periods in particular, there is very often little time to think; no time to think about the next gate or bend in the river. Fretting about any mistakes that have already been made and worrying about what might be round the next corner will be counter-productive. When in the middle of white water, like Haley, it is vital to be completely focused and in the moment, at one with the flow of the river. This ability to be completely present is also a key skill in other walks of life, and increasingly recognised as vital in business. It does not come naturally, however, and like sports men and women, business people can train to increase their skill in being present. In a world where the ability to 'multi-task' is increasingly being seen as a badge of honour amongst executives, the people who can focus exclusively, and not be distracted, will become the most valuable and cherished. Of course, it is important to be able to quickly and effectively switch from one issue or problem to another at short notice, but, at any given moment, if you want to be as effective as you can be, it is essential that you commit completely to the task at hand, and avoid distraction from competing issues.

'Mindfulness' techniques *(see Catherine McCanny's blog)* [Ref 18] are powerful in helping sports people achieve the level of absolute presence required to make split-second decisions while in the thick of the action; "do I pass or shoot?; come to the net or stay on the baseline?; paddle left or right?" Clearly, the best decisions would not be made if people were thinking about last week's game or off-field issues.

Understanding and recognising patterns and preferences, and using the language of 'riding the river', offers people a way to articulate their feelings more easily than they could otherwise. And knowing one's bank of preference when under pressure is a very useful first step in the self-awareness required in being able to deal with it, and invaluable in helping maintain the harmony and integration necessary to experience the rewards (and exhilaration) that come from getting in the flow.

CHAPTER TEN KEY LEARNING POINTS

- The role of Flow
- Optimal Performance
- Balance of Ability and Challenge
- Chaos vs Rigid banks
- Mindfulness

CHAPTER TEN REFLECTIONS

How often do you experience 'flow' in your everyday work? Do you expect to experience it? Capture some examples together with how it felt.

_____

_____

_____

_____

_____

_____

Are you regularly working at a level of challenge above or below your level of ability? How do you feel when you are? Recount examples of when you are as well as when you are not.

_____

_____

_____

_____

_____

_____

Which bank of the river do you find you bump against most often? Chaos or Rigid?   How do you recognise this (give some examples)?

_____

_____

_____

_____

_____

_____

_____

What behaviours do you see others around you display – withdraw/get busy/get irritated/worry? Anything else?

_____

_____

_____

_____

_____

_____

_____

Where are you when your phone beeps and vibrates during a meeting? Are you still in the room or has your attention moved elsewhere? List some examples when this has happened, together with an honest assessment of where your focus was.

_____

_____

_____

_____

_____

_____

Does your company culture reinforce and make a virtue of 'multi-tasking'? Think of some examples where this is the case and what impact it has.

_____

_____

_____

_____

_____

_____

Where does your motivation come from primarily?   List some of the main sources that come to mind.

_____

_____

_____

_____

_____

_____

_____

The Vital Edge

PART IV   SPORTING KNIGHTS

Leadership

No examination of sporting or business performance and achievement would be complete without acknowledging the critical role played by leaders. Leaders do of course come in all shapes, sizes and styles, and the science of leadership is a popular and worthwhile branch of study in and of itself.

The origins of the term 'Coach', as employed in today's business world, are to be found in the world of sport. Indeed, often, when I refer to myself as a coach, people make the assumption that I must be some sort of sports coach.

There have been many great leaders in sport, some who have adopted modern-day coaching approaches, some who lead with great authority, and some who are intellectual thinkers and integrate the latest scientific principles into their methods. All provide us with great insights that can be adopted or assimilated within other contexts, particularly business. I have chosen to look at three hugely successful, but quite different, sporting leaders, all of whom have made significant contributions to their respective sports.

Chapter Eleven   Identifying Talent

Sir Clive Woodward

I was honoured to be able to listen to Sir Clive Woodward, the British Olympic Association's Director of Elite Performance, speak during the build-up to the Olympic Games in London. Woodward is one of the world's leading and most-respected coaches, having led the England Rugby team to World Cup victory in 2003 in Australia. The most memorable nugget of wisdom he left me with was about what he looks for above all else when seeking to identify talent. It is what he calls the 'teachability' factor.

Is the person open and receptive to new information? Do they demonstrate a hunger for knowledge? Are they keen to learn? Assuming he was given a choice between two young people of similar current ability ('raw talent'), Woodward would always select the one with the highest teachability factor, even if they currently possessed a lower level of raw talent. This is a better indicator of future success at this stage of a young athlete's career, he would claim.

I recognise the importance of this factor in identifying talent and potential in the world of business too. Who are the people who are hungry, keen and interested? Who has a spark in their eye, a willingness to learn from every situation, and are a joy to work with? Another indicator these folks often display is a 'hunger' for feedback. Genuine talent does not feel that they 'know it all' already. They do not treat feedback at appraisal sessions as a challenge to their ability, but rather as a gift to help them improve.

Another major lesson that business could learn from the Olympics talent identification programme, is the way that potential is explored in people who are not currently actively engaged in a given sport. This often involves programmes of screening, inviting people to 'come and have a go' at a different sport, and actively watching people perform in 'adjacent' sports *(*e.g. could a fast rugby player make it as a sprinter, could a powerful swimmer with 'long levers' and large hands make a fantastic rower*)?* Approaches like these are becoming common-place in identifying future potential Olympic champions.

Businesses typically recruit and promote in a linear fashion, focusing only on the people who pass through their hands, or apply to join their department, thereafter fitting them into a pre-defined career framework. To identify and attract the best talent in the future, how about casting the net wider, actively scouting people in adjacent roles, and inviting people to 'come and have a go'?

Talent is a precious thing, and many businesses struggle to know how to identify, manage and nurture it. Should it be given 'maverick status', does it need to be controlled? Well, I guess the answer might well vary depending on the culture of the company, what period in the company's development it is at, or even what sort of leader is in charge?

I have played and watched football over more years than I care to remember, and the recurring debate about how teams should accommodate rare talent just never goes away. What I have seen is that teams who are riding on the crest of a wave, winning everything in sight, and blowing the opposition away, can often afford the luxury of the occasional maverick or outlier. Often described as a genius, these players entertain the crowds and keep the sports (and sometimes front-page) writers happy.

But, when the going gets tough, everyone is expected to put in a shift. Sulking on the wings with your hands on your hips, complaining about not getting good service, doesn't go down well – not with the crowd, team mates, or coach (as it wouldn't with your shareholders, colleagues, or boss). In fact, as the years have passed, I believe that even the very best of the modern day players in football (e.g. Cristiano Ronaldo or Leonel Messi) are not just geniuses with the ball and in attacking play, but they are industrious all over the pitch, supporting their defence when their team is without the ball. This could not always be said of 'great' players in the past, some of whom would see their job as done when the ball entered their own half, and would effectively rest until they regained possession.

It's a big issue for companies too. When someone is bestowed the title talent (or genius) – what is expected of them and of others? Are they to be lauded and treated differently? Do managers become fearful of losing them (perhaps to a rival company – perhaps even to another part of the same company)? Should we expect the same commitment and application from them as everyone else? As in football, it will depend on where the company is at, both culturally and developmentally. Start-ups are often hugely dependent on the creativity and innovative thinking of talented and driven individuals. These people may hang around long enough to see the fledgling company through the early years, but start to become bored by the workings of the enterprise scale operation. They typically hand over the reins of the more 'operational' activities to someone better equipped to do that job, allowing them to move on to the next big idea.

As with anything precious, making sure you nurture and develop talent is paramount, and always in the right direction. Leaders need to be clear about what it is that has marked them out, and find out what it is that they recognise in themselves that they feel needs to be expressed. There is nothing more disheartening than to see talent being identified, only to see it being squeezed through a 'one-size-fits-all' talent programme.

So, what might be useful approaches to adopt in dealing with and maximising the potential of talent in your business?

Encourage talented people to see the big picture   This way they will be even more powerful. While they may be content to delve down and go deeper into problem solving, their effectiveness can be expanded beyond limited boundaries by exposure to wider horizons.

Avoid talent becoming strangled by internal politics and self-interest   Try to use talented people for the good of the whole business. This might mean moving them round and giving them exposure to different areas. Watch out for managers along the way getting too reliant and possessive, and putting obstacles in the way of them moving on or being shared.

Beware the talent turning 'prima donna'   Like the football stars who can lose touch with reality, and are unwilling to do the dirty work when the team's backs are up against the wall, talent that is not made to feel part of the team, that does not share in the vision and goals, may feel they can stand on the sidelines shaking their head at the mess the rest of the team have got themselves into.

Avoid squeezing talent into pre-defined roles that strangle their innovation   Corporations can be over-obsessed with ensuring people follow particular career paths, and assuming these are the only ways to achieve a successful career. You may have to construct a totally new role to accommodate talent and ensure you get the best from them. I liken this to the best football coaches being able to adapt their team system and formation to permit the talented player to have a roving role that makes the most of their skills. Nothing frustrates talented players more than shoe-horning them into a rigid team formation, stifling their ability to express themselves and expecting them to work within strictly defined structures.

Look for ways to stretch and challenge talent to avoid them becoming bored   Bored talent will soon look elsewhere for their stimulation, so ensure they have the ability to work on multiple projects.

Reward talented people appropriately   What is the market paying? What would it cost to recruit and train someone else to reach the same level of effectiveness, should they up and leave? Is the reward commensurate with the contribution they are making to the company's success, or are they stuck in a pay structure that does not have the ability to recognise extraordinary contribution?

Avoid organisational friction   Watch out for talent that is ineffective at bringing other people with them, or is dismissive of people who they deem to be 'not as smart'. Nobody survives on their own, and the best talent is sensitive to the needs of others. Identify any potential difficulty like this early on, and do something about it, for the good of everyone.

Encourage knowledge sharing and collaboration   Provide opportunities for talent to be shadowed and for them to mentor other high-potential people. Develop a pipeline of talent and a knowledge base of intelligence, so that you are not over-exposed by the risk of sudden departures.

You and your business may be in a period where your teams are digging in, with backs to the wall and still trying to ride out the recession. There may be a distinct absence of flair on the field of play, but perhaps this is the very time that you need a 'match winner'. Football teams need a stroke of genius for someone to make the vital pass or score the decisive goal. Leaders in our companies and organisations are no different. They too need someone who can see the pass that others cannot see. They need different thinking, creative insights and people who dare to dream big. The leader's role is to nurture and cultivate the talent that is out there, blending it skilfully with the rest of the team, and encouraging the creation of opportunities for strokes of genius that will carve out the winning goals.

CHAPTER ELEVEN KEY LEARNING POINTS

- Talent Identification
- The 'teachability' factor
- Screening of adjacent disciplines for talent
- Stretch and challenge talent

CHAPTER ELEVEN REFLECTIONS

Does your organisation have a talent identification strategy? How is talent nurtured in your company?

_____

_____

_____

_____

_____

_____

_____

_____

Are your talented individuals treated as / or looked upon as elite and special? In what sort of ways?

_____

_____

_____

_____

_____

_____

_____

Are talented people moved around the business in order to gain wide-exposure, or are they utilised in a narrowly-focused area of speciality? List examples of how they are used.

_____

_____

_____

_____

_____

_____

_____

Is your organisation losing its talent to other more ambitious rivals? What are the costs of this?

_____

_____

_____

_____

_____

_____

_____

Are you actively looking for talent from other work areas? What sources are possible?

_____

_____

_____

_____

_____

_____

_____

Chapter Twelve   Half-Time Pep Talks

Sir Alex Ferguson

Another sporting *'Sir'* who has contributed a lifetime to leadership and coaching, this time in the world of football, is Sir Alex Ferguson. Those of you familiar with Ferguson will be aware of his reputation for no-nonsense management. He is often talked about as an old-fashioned manager, the last of his generation. A Scot, from the Govan area of Glasgow, his style could never be described as soft or fluffy, but there is clearly more to his approach than the oft-cited 'hair-dryer treatment' (alluding to a steady, loud tirade) that he has been known to mete out to players on occasions.

I was lucky enough to attend a coaching course, run by the Scottish Football Association, at their Inverclyde HQ in Largs, where Ferguson was on the senior coaching staff. It was fascinating to watch the real man (as opposed to the public persona) close up. He had a unique, almost child-like, approach, always looking to make things fun. In the evenings he would organise quizzes and games, always with an ultra-competitive edge. Although part of the old school of football management, having played in the 1960s, he was always open to the benefits and opportunities that modern techniques could provide, and was in the vanguard of managers willing to experiment with new methods.

Damian Hughes (*author of Liquid Leadership, 2009*) [Ref 19], spent time close to Sir Alex, researching and interviewing for his book. He described one half-time situation when Manchester United came off the pitch losing 2-0, having put in a fairly inept first-half performance. Believers of the Ferguson myth would assume that cups would fly, and his face would turn a deep shade of purple. Instead, what Hughes described, was a very calm dressing room, where, first of all, Ferguson set the leadership tone. He reminded the players how good they were, and what they were capable of. He then acknowledged that the team was in a difficult position in the match, but that he had every belief in their ability to get themselves out of it and turn the game around. He then asked them to calmly speak up and tell him, and share with each other, what they felt they needed to do differently in the second half. He then sat back and listened without interruption. Before the team went back on to the field, he said that he wouldn't disagree, and that it sounded like a good plan. He reiterated the faith he had in their ability, and simply asked them to go out and do what they said they would do. They won 3-2.

Ferguson, in this instance, demonstrated some very important principles of leadership. He provided vision and direction, he trusted his players to know what they needed to do, he listened to them and gave them a voice, and he handed back responsibility by allowing them to implement their own plan. People are more engaged when they feel ownership and responsibility. Imagine how damaging it could have been had he made a charade of listening, only to then rubbish what they had to say and impose a plan of his own? Integrity of values and behaviour would have been shattered, and future trust and respect would have been damaged.

I have no doubt, on occasions, Sir Alex has resorted to the 'hair-dryer' strategy, but not as frequently as his reputation would have us think, or as often as the tabloids would like us to believe. From players who have worked closely with Ferguson over the years, they highlight that he was highly tuned to which players would respond to his infamous robust style, and which were more likely to respond to an arm around the shoulder and a quiet word of encouragement.

One of the world's biggest authorities on the science and art of leadership is Ronald Heifetz. He is author of some of the most persuasive books on the pitfalls and enablers of great leadership. He makes some very sound arguments about leadership being about challenging the way things are, but that any attempt to challenge things that people hold dear, such as habits, routines and traditions, will be met with strong feelings, opposition, and, on occasions, even aggression. Leading does involve disturbing people, putting provocative ideas out there, and challenging people to face tough realities. However, skilled leaders also know the importance of getting people to take responsibility for solving their own problems. Leaders who get seduced by people's appeals to do the fixing for them, to come up with the answers for them, and to take all the tough decisions, are doing both themselves and their people a major disservice. Themselves, because ultimately they will be blamed when things do not work out, and the people, because they will have been robbed of a chance to grow, learn and adapt.

Heifetz & Linsky, in *Leadership on the Line (2002)* [Ref 20], highlight some of the key behaviours that mark out excellent leaders from ineffective leaders.

Go beyond your Authority When people are elected to office or hired into post, it is seldom part of the job description to make life difficult for everyone. The expectation is that they will come up with good answers and not confront people with difficult choices. So, one of the first challenges a new leader faces is going beyond their authority to do just that, and to get people to face up to and tackle the problems they face.

Get on the balcony Leaders need to get and maintain perspective. In the midst of the action on the field, when people are in the thick of the action, leaders benefit from observing the big picture from the balcony or grandstand, allowing them to make and suggest adjustments to strategy or tactics.

Orchestrate the conflict   All major change, or tackling of substantial and complex issues, will involve varying levels of conflict. Heifetz & Linsky propose four key ways that conflict can be orchestrated effectively.

Create a holding environment   This is a space (virtual or physical, e.g. the dressing room) within which tough, divisive issues can be tackled. It may be a space with rules and a common language that allow concerns to be aired without threat.

Control the temperature   Heat is inevitably generated when significant change is proposed. Indeed, part of a leader's job is to ensure there is enough heat, as, without a certain level of distress, people are unlikely to feel compelled to take any action. Ferguson was certainly renowned for being capable of 'generating heat' – his 'hairdryer' treatment of screaming at players at close quarters is legendary. But the leader also needs to gauge when the heat is too high, and find ways to temporarily cool things down. Methods can include temporarily taking some more of the responsibility, or using humour, or arrange a time-out or social gathering.

Pace the work   Recognising the rate at which people can absorb change is an important skill of leadership. It is also a very risky aspect of leadership in its own right. For every person who agrees that the pace needs to be relaxed slightly, there will be someone who wants to push on at a faster rate. It is important that progress is not 'stopped' completely, but rather adjustments to the agenda of change are made clear, so that everyone can see that progress is still being made, and people are being mentally prepared for some of the harder tasks that lie ahead.

Show them the future Regular reminders of the positive vision of the future are necessary to help people through tough periods of change. If it is possible to demonstrate small steps that are being taken toward the destination then do so, as it helps make tangible the reality of the vision.

Finally – Give the work back Fixing problems for other people, will, at best, provide short-term relief. Issues will surface again, perhaps in another guise, and people will be no better equipped than before to deal with them.

Ferguson certainly displayed a number of these principles in the half-time session described in this chapter. He established the holding environment using his authority to set the ground rules, controlled the temperature by calmly stating some observations as he had observed them 'from the balcony', but ultimately did what all great leaders do, handed responsibility back to the people who are best placed to solve the problem.

CHAPTER TWELVE KEY LEARNING POINTS

- Leadership tone
- Controlling the temperature
- Getting on the balcony
- Handing back responsibility

CHAPTER TWELVE REFLECTIONS

How effective are the leaders within your organisation? In what way could they be more effective? Do they receive coaching on their leadership?

_____

_____

_____

_____

_____

_____

How engaged are the workforce in the company's purpose, vision and direction? If they're not engaged, what prevents full engagement?

_____

_____

_____

_____

_____

_____

_____

Does everyone in your area of work feel that they have a voice, and that they will be heard?   List some ways that is made possible.

How consistent is the culture of the organisation in terms of its integrity, values and behaviours? Think of ways in which that is demonstrated.

_____

_____

_____

_____

_____

_____

_____

Chapter Thirteen   Marginal Gains

Sir David Brailsford

Yet another sporting knight who has had a significant impact on the world of sport is Sir David Brailsford. David is the Performance Director of British Cycling and the Manager of Team Sky, the team that produced the winner of the Tour de France in 2012 and 2013. He was also in charge of the British cycling teams that have dominated the world of cycling in the past 5 or 6 years, including the Beijing and London Olympics.

A quiet, unassuming man, he has made the term 'aggregation of marginal gains' one of the hottest topics in the world of sport. His services have been in demand from many other sports, all of whom are keen to apply his methods, to see if they too might benefit in the way that cycling clearly has. So, what is so special about the marginal gains philosophy? Well, in typically modest fashion, Brailsford plays it down and describes it simply as meticulous planning and attention to detail.

If you take absolutely everything you can think of that could impact on a cycling performance, and you make just a 1% improvement on each element, when all of these elements are then put back together again, the net effect of all of the marginal improvements can add up to a significant improvement in performance. But, that barely starts to touch on the level of detail applied under Brailsford's leadership. After all, every ambitious athlete, in any sport is also trying to stretch their ability and performance by small margins through combinations of advanced training, nutrition, rest and psychology. So, what is so special about Brailsford's approach? It is that he has left no stone unturned in searching for the gains that get converted into 'the vital edge' required to become number one. He has gone beyond the obvious fitness and nutrition improvements (they are givens!) and included areas such as biomechanics, personal hygiene, sleep posture, air conditioning in hotel rooms, as well as a 'secret squirrel' research and development unit.

His obsession with hygiene makes sense when you consider how important it is for athletes to train to a meticulously planned schedule in order to achieve peak performance at just the right time. Every sick day in a year that interrupts that schedule is a contributor to a potential degradation in peak performance. So, attention to hand-washing techniques is key in Brailsford's teams in order to minimise the chances of contracting any unwanted germs. A similar level of detail is applied to ensuring the riders have a consistent and familiar night's sleep during the course of a tour when they are sleeping in a different hotel every night. Teams of 'bedroom preparers' are sent ahead to set up air conditioning units to create precisely the right air quality for a good night's sleep, replace bed linen with hypo-allergenic linen, and replace the hotel pillows with each rider's own unique pillow to ensure they have the right sleeping posture, avoiding any stiff necks as they set off on the next day's race.

And, it's not just the riders who are expected to make marginal gains in all areas. The mechanical support teams, for example, can make small contributions to improved performance by finding more creative ways to replace bikes, change wheels, and otherwise keep the riders on the road. Drivers of support vehicles look at ways of issuing instructions sharper. Drink and food distributors find marginally more efficient ways to get supplies to the riders when needed. It all adds up, and any one of these could make the winning difference.

Away from day to day racing, the 'secret squirrel' team are looking constantly at industry developments that might improve equipment such as helmets, clothing or the bikes themselves. By staying close to advances in metal technology or fabric improvements, and working with scientists to find an extra edge on the aerodynamics of the bicycle frame, this team too are looking for their 1% gain.

Brailsford describes his style of leadership as being like an orchestra conductor. Not actually playing any instrument himself, but setting the rhythm, the pace, the tone, and keeping all units of the operation working together. And is there any proof that this attention to detail works? Well, *The Tour* in 2012 was won by

Bradley Wiggins by a mere 3 minutes, or 0.05% of a total race time of more than 87 hours. And, the margin of victory when Victoria Pendleton took gold in the Women's Olympic Kierin final at London was almost imperceptible, until the race was replayed on TV in slow-motion.

There is much for business leaders to learn from Brailsford and his methods (*Brailsford, Dave, A Winning Advantage, Sky Pro Cycling, 2010,* [Ref 3], as his principles are of as much relevance to the world of work as they are to sport. So, what are some of the key issues for leaders to be aware of?

Room for improvement   There is always room to improve, no matter how well people believe a job is being done. As Brailsford himself says, "If a mechanic sticks a tyre on, and someone comes along and says it could be done better, it's not an insult – it's because we are always striving for improvement, in absolutely every single thing we do."

Welcome feedback   Following on from above, instilling a culture where everyone is 'feedback hungry' is one of the greatest gifts a leader can encourage. Not just being open to feedback, but actively seeking it, is key to learning, and is closely aligned to Sir Clive Woodward's 'teachability' factor that we touched on in chapter 11.

Strategy & execution   Successfully applying the marginal gains approach is dependent on everyone being clear on the principles, understanding the approach and buying into it completely. To achieve this, leaders need to display passion, conviction and clarity of direction, as well as create a clear vision of success that everyone wants to be part of. As we have seen from the cycling examples, some of the aspects may appear trivial in isolation (e.g. hand-washing techniques), but are an essential part of the bigger picture.

Discipline & commitment   The cyclists in Brailsford's team clearly wanted to succeed, and were determined to stick to the discipline and sacrifices associated with the plan. This would not have been successful if Brailsford had to constantly gain commitment from everyone to execute the next stage of the plan. The key was the 'internal commitment' displayed by everyone. They were doing it for themselves, they wanted to do it, they wanted the rewards, and they did not need to be constantly bought into the vision.

CHAPTER THIRTEEN KEY LEARNING POINTS

- Aggregation of 'marginal gains'
- The winning edge
- Continuous improvement
- Importance of feedback
- Strategy & execution
- Discipline & commitment

CHAPTER THIRTEEN REFLECTIONS

How does your company demonstrate a desire for continuous improvement? Even when projects have gone well, are lessons for improvement sought out as a matter of course? List some ways this has been done.

_____

_____

_____

_____

_____

_____

How 'feedback hungry' is your organisation? Is feedback reserved for performance review sessions (quarterly/annually)? Does it give rise to defensive reactions? Write down examples.

_____

_____

_____

_____

_____

_____

_____

How well equipped are managers, in your experience, to deliver constructive feedback, and encourage constructive conversations? What could be improved?

_____

_____

_____

_____

_____

_____

_____

How much 'internal commitment' do you observe in your company? Do people need to be reminded/asked again regularly or are they bought in to executing plans and achieving strategy? Consider any examples where this is done well or badly.

_____

_____

_____

_____

_____

_____

How much do you exploit all the sources of learning available on the outside of your organisation and even outside your industry? In what ways might this be exploited further?

_____

_____

_____

_____

_____

_____

_____

The Vital Edge

PART V   GOING BEYOND LIMITS

So far we have been using experiences from a variety of sports to explore connections and learnings that can be taken into the world of business, and indeed into personal development too. On the whole these sports are ones that many can relate to, and perhaps even have participated in at some stage of their lives. We may not have experienced the dizzy heights of Olympic Gold medal winners or Wimbledon champions, but that does not prevent us having some inkling of how it must feel, or what inner voices might have to be confronted at match point or as we stand over a winning putt.

There are of course a small number of men and women who choose to go beyond what most mere mortals would consider as healthy, safe or even as sport. What, if anything, is there to learn from these thrill seekers, adrenaline junkies and explorers whose idea of a good time is to go way beyond normal limits?

Chapter Fourteen   Riding on the Edge

How low can you go?

Imagine yourself riding a motorcycle in a high-speed race. You are at full throttle going round the final bend. Only a delicate balance between gravity and centrifugal forces are preventing you from flying off the track. At that moment, are you in control of your bike, or are you out of control? The answer is you are right on the edge. Too in control, and you probably aren't taking enough risk, and are unlikely to win the race. Too out of control and the likelihood is you are in for a very painful crash.

In 2013, at age 20, Marc Márquez of Spain became the youngest ever World Champion of MotoGP in the final race of the season in Valencia. For anyone who hasn't witnessed MotoGP, it is truly breath-taking. Riders appear to defy gravity on the bends, with their knees and elbows scraping the surface of the track at speeds in excess of 300km/hour. Experts have commented on the young Márquez's style saying, "….he drags his elbow on every corner and leans his body and bike closer to the ground than any of his rivals." In this sport, being daring and aggressive is a requirement if you hope to succeed. It would look as though an ability to shut out thoughts of fear and consequences of getting it wrong are a necessity. Yet, at the same time, knowing, in that instant, just what would be too much, too fast, too risky, is clearly also a vital (and life-preserving) requirement. As is resilience, perseverance and the ability to learn from (and not be put off by) misjudgements.

During the course of the season, Marquez also set the record for the highest-speed crash in motorcycle racing. While practicing his gravity-defying turns, he lost control at 320km/hour. He managed to throw himself from his bike just before it crashed against a concrete wall. He was catapulted into a gravel safety trap at 280km/hour, walked away, and competed in the race the next day. He was very clear about the fact that he must keep learning and improving. (*The Sydney Morning Herald, Nov 17 2013*) [Ref 21]. In the final race of the season, he needed to finish no worse than fourth to secure the title. He worked out that keeping his two main rivals in front of him, where he could watch their every move, was a better strategy than having them plot and scheme their moves from behind him. He rode a sensible, calculating race, taking less risks, staying out of trouble, and safely securing third place, sufficient to win the World Championship.

In your life, would you describe yourself as in control or out of control? Or, have you found just the right balance – not just for you, but for your teams, your colleagues, and for your organisation? Are you pushing the limits constantly, in order to win the race, and, as a result, and, as a consequence, are you in danger of occasionally spinning out of control? Or, are you driving a safe race, within the pack, within your comfort zone, making sure you finish, but never in danger of winning? What about the people you see around you? Do you recognise and distinguish the cruisers and the risk takers?

The reality of course is that people vary across time and situation. No-one can sustain flat-out, full-throttle, in what they do, without crashing sooner or later (probably sooner!). Everyone needs time for recovery and regeneration, and cruise time (or even a pit stop) is a sensible way to achieve that. There will of course be times when the prize is considered worth it, when the risks are deemed to be in your favour, and you decide to go for it. The skill is in the judgement of picking your moment, selecting when best to make your move, and being aware of what you can actually influence, and what is actually within your control.

Control is one of the most regular themes that I find crops up when coaching business clients. Some people report that they feel they have no control. They may be in a job where they are not given the responsibility they feel they deserve, they are not involved in making decisions, they believe they are unable to challenge authority. They feel they have more to offer, but don't seem to be able to get their voice heard. They have a sense of being trapped and helpless.

Others feel out of control. Things are moving too fast, they are expected to make the key decisions, they don't feel they have the support around them to share the burden, they are in authority and therefore 'expected' to be able to handle the pace and responsibility.

Yet others, may have moved beyond a simple wish for control, to a state of not being able to 'let go' of control. They retain a tight grasp on the tiller, perhaps fearing that their very identity and existence depends on maintaining this position. Any suggestion of circumstances changing can cause panic, resulting in them tightening their control even more.

The reality is that control is 'illusory'. We believe we can control more of our lives than we actually can. **Sandra Sanger's short article** *'The Illusion of Control'* is worth a read on this subject [Ref 22]. Excessive control can cause damage to both individuals and to organisations. Control also stifles creative thinking and innovation (for a balanced argument on this point see **Busco, Frigo, Giavannoni & Maraghini, Control vs Creativity, Strategic Finance, August 2012)**, [Ref 23]. It diminishes trust and openness, vital conditions required for healthy workplace engagement.

The irony is that there may actually be more control enjoyed in adopting a flexible position than working constantly at keeping everything just so. Adopting this stance, will of course call for many people to re-frame their concept of control. Those who play sports, such as golf or tennis, know this intuitively. Smooth and controlled golf swings and tennis strokes, rarely occur as a result of intense concentration on every minutiae of the grip, stance and swing. A relaxed, flexible and natural approach, as generated by a state of 'flow' (see Chapter 10) is more likely to produce successful outcomes – resulting in greater overall control of your golf, tennis, or business performance.

Recognising how little we actually do control in our lives is a great starting point to allow us to re-appraise our relationship with control. Being consciously selective with the energy we choose to expend on those areas where it is really worth pushing to the edge, requires flexibility and recognition of what areas you really can influence.

CHAPTER FOURTEEN KEY LEARNING POINTS

- Riding on the edge
- Taking risks
- Levels of control
- What can you control or influence?
- Flexibility

CHAPTER FOURTEEN REFLECTIONS

What don't you control? You can think about this in terms of work or your life in general.

_____

_____

_____

_____

_____

_____

_____

What have you been trying to control? Either in relation to work or your life in general.

_____

_____

_____

_____

_____

_____

_____

What could you influence that you have not been?

_____

_____

_____

_____

_____

_____

_____

What actually happens when you give up control? Give examples where you recall doing so. If you haven't tried, what areas are candidates to experiment with?

_____

_____

_____

_____

_____

_____

Chapter Fifteen   Exploration

Skiing Antartica solo

Felicity Aston, a young woman from Kent in England, set out in 2012 to cross the Antartic alone on skis. This is a distance of 1,744km (over 1,000 miles), carrying 85kg of supplies at temperatures of -30°C (-22°F). Starting out on 25th November, the epic journey would take 59 days. In so doing, Felicity became the first woman to ski across Antartica unaccompanied. Her account of the monotonous and hostile landscape is chilling. She recalls, with great honesty, her fears and doubts, and the extreme loneliness of the experience. She thinks about where her motivation for taking on such a task came from, and what it was that drove her on day after day. She highlights perseverance as perhaps the key quality, especially at times when under severe pressure. She also highlights how vitally important the mental preparation for her journey was, stating that "Polar exploration is as much about what is going on in your head as anything else."

Felicity used visualisation and mindfulness techniques to prepare for what she would encounter. She was aware of the monotony of the landscape, the way that sky and land merge such that you cannot see any horizon, and the tricks that can play with the mind. She rehearsed, over and over, in her mind, how she would feel, what she would be doing, what she would be focusing on (e.g. her heartbeat, her breathing, rustling of her clothing). *(Felicity Aston website,* [Ref 24]*)*

But why? Why take on such extreme challenges at all? To answer this, we need to look deeper into our neurobiological makeup and how we as humans arrived at where we are today on an evolutionary level. Exploration is a fundamental aspect of what has made us human. It has been important to our societies and human advancement for thousands of years. It is all about asking ourselves questions. *What is over there? What is on the other side of that hill?* The basic principle of science is about exploration, asking questions, making assumptions to be tested, experimenting with a view to disproving hypotheses, and ultimately advancing human knowledge about our universe.

But this doesn't fully explain why people take on hazardous tasks that could risk their life. After all, that sounds counter-intuitive as a successful strategy for evolution. However, humans have clearly not survived, adapted and been so successful, in evolutionary terms, by being non-curious, non-exploratory or risk averse. There has no doubt been selection that has favoured those who have reached out, explored new territories, sought new ways of living, and have learned from all of this new experience. We are not all polar explorers, and nor do we all sign up to bungee-jump, but we are all familiar with the frisson of excitement associated with any number of activities that even mildly take us closer to the edge.

This may be a fairground ride, watching a horror movie or climbing to the top of a hill and enjoying the view, as well as the sense of achievement. The closer we draw to this 'edge', and it will be quite different and personal for each individual, the more our senses are awakened, the more alert (even alive) we become.

And what relevance does this have for business, and for our own personal development? Well, it is when we get closer to the edge of things that the conditions for change are most favourable. As we get close to the edge of our understanding, our uncertainty levels increase. As things become less predictable, we seek knowledge that will help us to restore order. It is at this leading edge that learning occurs, when we make new neural connections within our brain. It can be experienced dramatically as 'aha' moments, or over a longer period of time as new neural networks become reinforced and strengthened, and older pathways become disused and atrophy.

Skilful leaders and coaches use this to the advantage of their people and clients, by posing questions and setting them challenges. The source of creativity and innovation in our businesses emanates from people making connections, building on existing knowledge and stretching their thinking into new territories. I like to think of coaching as like an exploration of the mind, instead of discovering polar territory, the exploration is of motivations, values, drives, beliefs and assumptions. Coaching is aided by tools like questioning and listening. The exploring in a coaching relationship is being done by the client, the coach is merely the prompter, asking questions like "what is over there?", "what might you find if you looked on the other side of that assumption?" or "how is that belief serving your expedition?" The coach is the expedition aide and the support vehicle. The client is the explorer.

The final word goes to Felicity Aston who said, "If you can just find a way to keep going...whether you're running a marathon, facing financial problems, have bad news to deliver, or it's tough at work. If you can just find a way to keep going, then you will discover that you have potential within yourself that you never realised…For me, sometimes I will be sitting in my tent in the morning bawling my eyes out….It's not been pretty. But I've kept going, and that is the important thing, because at some point in the future you'll look back and just be amazed at how far you've come."

CHAPTER FIFTEEN KEY LEARNING POINTS

- Perseverance
- Mental preparation
- Exploration as a change and learning exercise
- Coaching as exploration

CHAPTER FIFTEEN REFLECTIONS

What territory (or territories) are you exploring?

_____

_____

_____

_____

_____

_____

_____

Where is / What is the next big 'learning edge' for you?

What role does exploration play in your business? How is it encouraged and reinforced? Give some examples.

_____

_____

_____

_____

_____

_____

_____

_____

What happens when you cannot see the horizon / bigger picture / over the next hill?   How do you feel personally?   What do you do?

_____

_____

_____

_____

_____

_____

How does your business ensure people are challenged to 'find their edge'? Provide some examples of how this is done. If it isn't, provide some ways it could be.

_____

_____

_____

_____

_____

_____

_____

How is coaching used in your organisation to help people explore their landscape and make discoveries? Which areas? If not used, which areas/people could benefit?

_____

_____

_____

_____

_____

_____

_____

What qualities are valued in your business? Curiosity, exploration, perseverance, resilience?

The Vital Edge

The Final Whistle

So, what have we discovered on this journey through sporting anecdote and metaphor?

For some people, perhaps the stories will stay with you, and provide a useful connection to allow you to think about your own performance, your team's performance, or your entire organisation's performance.

For others, the opportunity to reflect and capture responses to the 'ponder' questions in each chapter may have triggered new ways of thinking about how you will approach things differently in the future.

Others will be intrigued by the potential for use within teams, using the stories to elicit responses to questions, and posing the 'ponder' questions to generate group discussion and create interaction and dialogue amongst people.

****

We have seen performances played out both by teams and by individuals. Team performance is more than a simple summation of the individual contributions. The significant, though often elusive role played by collaboration, inter-personal, and intra-team dynamics, as well as the sacrifices individuals are prepared to make for the team, are all key ingredients in any team's success.

We explored the world inside the heads of athletes, and noted how readily techniques for being mentally prepared can be adopted by anyone outside of sport. The power of visualisation, long exploited by sportspeople, can be extremely useful in everyday situations. In business, it can be invaluable. Mental rehearsal of presentations, negotiations, interviews and one to one meetings. This is more than simply running through a check-list of notes in advance to make sure you have your facts straight. Great visualisation employs all the senses, the layout of the room, the general ambience and background noises, the smell of the room, the temperature, as well as incorporating props like lecterns, notes and furniture layout. Even rehearsing your feelings and emotions in advance by considering how you 'want to be' when situations arise.

We also looked at the damage that can be caused by the 'inner voice' that we all experience from time to time. Some people refer to this as their 'inner critic'; coaches often refer to it as the 'gremlin'. Dr.Steve Peters, the psychologist to Team GB, calls this 'irrational' interference the 'Chimp'. Many top sportspeople, including the cyclists Vicky Pendleton, Chris Hoy and Bradley Wiggins, all Olympic cycling gold medallists, have adopted the Chimp concept as a way of encapsulating their inner voices, feelings and emotions. The ones that tend to creep into consciousness at times of doubt and which are certainly not helpful. The Chimp may show up in any number of destructive ways, mocking, laughing, criticising, distracting, which, left undealt with, can lead to self-doubt, self-criticism and even self-loathing. By giving this collection of feelings a name and a shape (such as Chimp – or you can create your own!) it allows athletes to recognise it more easily when it appears, to tame it, by taking control of it, and not allowing it to take over. This of course takes practice, but many top performers swear by the technique. [Ref 25]

Our exploration of barriers that previously were considered insurmountable demonstrated the important role of motivation. What is it about people who refuse to believe that getting over obstacles cannot be achieved? What differentiates their approach to others who give up all too soon? When people give up, they are often closer to achieving their goal than they realise. Think about that. If you knew that it was only going to take one more try, or that you were only minutes away from a breakthrough in thinking, would you keep right on going? Perhaps just looking at the situation from a different perspective, and not considering it a problem at all, is what is required. In the early days of Henry Ford creating his automobile empire, he had reached a stage where production could not keep up with demand. He called a meeting with all of his senior and longest-serving team. Many of them had been with him from the earliest days, and knew the production line and its operation inside out. He asked them what needed to be done to get the production line to go faster. One by one they each dismissed the possibility. They were running flat out. Nothing could make it go faster. Exasperated by their lack of vision and ambition, Ford is reputed to have terminated the meeting by shouting out, "Go find me a 19 year old who doesn't know it can't go any faster!"

We have also discovered the advantages an optimistic outlook uncovers, especially when combined with a positive, permanent and pervasive explanatory style for good events. Possessing this powerful mix of outlook and style will often bridge any gap in talent between two individuals, and will certainly be a huge differentiator between two people of equivalent raw talent. Perhaps this combination is close to what Clive Woodward refers to as 'teachability', the magic ingredient he seeks when identifying talent.

The critical role of leadership and the different ways it can influence performance was explored through the eyes of three very different sporting leaders. As well as recognising, and subsequently nurturing talent, leaders also have a huge role to play in handing back responsibility to people, so that they feel more committed to take action, that their learning is more enduring, and that they grow and develop as individuals in their own right, perhaps into the next generation of leaders. We also saw how important the role of leadership can be in seeking new methods and insights, being sufficiently humble to look for answers outside immediate spheres of expertise (Henry Ford's request once again comes to mind), and to constantly be seeking 'marginal gains' that make the winning difference in any competitive environment.

Finally, we touched on what compels some exceptional people to go beyond normal limits; to seek new territories; to stretch further than many might say is sensible or safe. This raised interesting questions about what it means to be 'in control'. In our everyday business lives, we are seldom in mortal danger, yet many cling to safe, risk-averse strategies. What scope is there for giving up some control, and what opportunities might emerge from that? To what extent does your business need to keep exploring, discovering and innovating? What mind-sets will be required to help make that happen?

****

To the very best athletes, a well prepared brain is every bit as vital to ensuring peak performance as finely-tuned muscles. In the case of the corporate athlete it is the most important asset they have. It is the brain where the inner game is played. Where motivation and desire is seeded, nourished by optimism and hope. Top performances are not best left to luck and chance. Training, skills development, and above all, mental preparation are essential if you want to give of your best. Our corporations, businesses, and organisations, are demanding and challenging arenas within which we are expected to perform. You can be part of the new breed of corporate athlete emerging; equipped to face those challenges with vigour; capable of performing in the face of adversity; knowing you can handle tough situations; resilient to disappointment; always prepared to step out beyond accepted limits, and to seek that vital edge.

Good luck on your journey.

Let the games begin!

The Vital Edge

References

[Ref 1] Gallwey, Tim, The Inner Game of Work, 2000

[Ref 2] Gallwey, Tim, The Inner Game of Tennis, 1975

[Ref 3] Brailsford, Dave, A Winning Advantage, Sky Pro Cycling, 2010, http://www.teamsky.com/article/0,27290,17547_5792058,00.html

[Ref 4] Dick, Frank, With thanks to Frank Dick for bringing this story to my attention, http://www.frankdick.co.uk/

[Ref 5] General Electric (GE) Innovation Barometer, 2012 http://www.ge.com/innovationbarometer/downloads.html

[Ref 6] Kilmann, Ralph, Thomas-Kilmann Conflict Mode Instrument, http://www.kilmanndiagnostics.com/overview-thomas-kilmann-conflict-mode-instrument-tki

[Ref 7] McDermott, Steve, How to be a complete and utter failure in life, work and everything, 2002

[Ref 8] McTaggart, Lynne. The Intention Experiment. Harper Element, London, 2007

[Ref 9] Brann, Amy, Make Your Brain Work, 2013

[Ref 10] Doidge, Norman, The Brain that Changes Itself, 2007

[Ref 11] Warne, Shane, Avoiding the Yips, 2013, http://www.thesportingedge.co.uk/blog_article.asp?ArticleID=29#sthash.KaRydipe.dpuf

[Ref 12] Seligman, Martin E.P., Learned Optimism, 2006 (page 163)

[Ref 13] Karageorghis,C.I. & Terry,P.C., Inside Sport Psychology, 2011

[Ref 14] Romero, Rebecca, BBC Olympic Blog (August 2008): http://www.bbc.co.uk/blogs/olympics/2008/08/the_demons_that_drive_romero.html

[Ref 15] Pink, Dan, The Puzzle of Motivation, T*ED talk, 2009*, http://www.ted.com/talks/dan_pink_on_motivation.html

[Ref 16] Daniels, Haley, Personal Blog, http://haleydaniels.blogspot.co.uk/2013/05/national-team-trials-2013.html, May 2013

[Ref 17] Siegel, Dan, Mindsight, The New Science of Personal Transformation, 2010

[Ref 18] McCanny, Catherine, The Application of Mindfulness Practice to Sport, http://www.thesportinmind.com/articles/the-application-of-mindfulness-practice-to-sport/

[Ref 19] Hughes, Damian, Liquid Leadership, 2009

[Ref 20] Heifetz, R & Linsky, M, Leadership on the Line (2002)

[Ref 21] The Sydney Morning Herald, Nov 17 2013, http://www.smh.com.au/sport/motorsport/marc-marquez-makes-motogp-history-20131116-2xnfw.html#ixzz2kzxyrI2p

[Ref 22] Sanger, Sandra, 'The Illusion of Control', http://blog.sandrasanger.com/2011/09/22/the-illusion-of-control/).

[Ref 23] Busco, Frigo, Giavannoni & Maraghini, Control vs Creativity, Strategic Finance, August 2012, http://www.imanet.org/PDFs/Public/SF/2012_08/08_2012_frigo.pdf

[Ref 24] Aston, Felicity, Website, http://www.felicityaston.co.uk/

[Ref 25] Peters, Dr Steve, The Chimp Paradox, The Mind Management Programme for Confidence, Success and Happiness, 2011

[Ref 26] Csikszentmihalyi, M, Flow; The classic work on how to achieve happiness, 2002

About the author

Louis Collins is a coach and leadership development consultant to executives and board-level leaders across a wide range of global businesses. His career roles have been varied, including University Teaching Fellow, Executive within the Civil Service, and Director of Client Services within the Global Telecoms sector. He graduated with a science degree from the University of Glasgow and has a Ph.D. in psychology from the University of Wales, Cardiff. His background in science and psychology influence his approach to coaching and leadership development, by borrowing from models and theories of behaviour and neuroscience. To discover more about Louis and his approach to leadership coaching, visit www.gyroconsulting.com.

Feedback on the content of this book is greatly appreciated. Please submit any comments you would like to share through the website at www.gyroconsulting.com/contact-us.

If you are interested in following up on any of the ideas within the book, or developing them further through coaching or leadership development within your organisation, please send your contact details via the same route on the website www.gyroconsulting.com/contact-us.

www.ingramcontent.com/pod-product-compliance
Lightning Source LLC
Chambersburg PA
CBHW032006170526
45157CB00002B/569